P9-EDN-269

UNDERSTANDING THE SCOTS

UNDERSTANDING THE SCOTS

A GUIDE FOR SOUTH BRITONS AND OTHER FOREIGNERS

by

MORAY McLAREN

BELL PUBLISHING
NEW YORK

Library of Congress Catalog Card Number: 74-78955

This edition is published by Bell Publishing Company
a division of Crown Publishers, Inc.
by arrangement with Impulse Publications, Ltd.
b c d e f g h
Manufactured in the United States of America

CONTENTS

Chapter One : WHO ARE THE SCOTS? 7

Chapter Two : THE HIGHLANDER AND THE LOWLANDER 13

Chapter Three : THE PLEASURES AND CIVILITIES 41

Chapter Four : LANGUAGE AND OTHER DIFFERENCES 59

Chapter Five : THE SCOT ABROAD AND AT HOME 80

Chapter Six : THE BURNS CULT AND BONNIE-PRINCE-CHARLEYISM, ETC. 96

Chapter Seven : THE GREAT CITY RIVALRY 109

Chapter Eight : PURITANISM AND 'HIVING-OFF' 127

Chapter Nine : A MAN'S A MAN FOR A' THAT 138

Chapter Ten : NATIONALISM 152

CONTENTS

[illegible]

[illegible]

[illegible]

[illegible]

[illegible]

[illegible]

[illegible]

[illegible]

[illegible]

[illegible]

Chapter One

Who are the Scots?

THE first thing to understand about the Scots is that they are not English. This may seem a somewhat unnecessary statement for most of my own compatriots and for many English, particularly those living in the North of England. But it is a point worth making for a number of foreign visitors to these shores who are inclined to think of this main island of ours, with its adjacent archipelago of nearly a thousand other islands, as England, and of all the inhabitants as English.

The second thing to understand is that the Scots are not British, neither are the English (no self-respecting Englishman calls himself a Briton—does he?). Nor, for that matter, is anyone British. A Briton and British were uneasy terms disinterred after centuries to get round an awkward corner of description when the Parliaments of England and Scotland were united in 1707. But apart from George III who, poor man, before he went mad, went about the place, gutturally and proudly proclaiming himself to be the 'first King born a Briton', the terms didn't take on.

For some time, it is true, the English called Scotland North Britain, and in my own lifetime I have received letters from English friends addressed to me on the envelope at 'Edinburgh, N.B.'. This has invariably been effectively countered and stopped by replying with letters addressed to 'London, S.B.'.

The truth is that the best and most distinctive things in Britain are not British. Cricket is an English game, and no matter how many Scots, Welsh or Irish may be playing in it, the national team is the All England Eleven. Shakespeare is an English poet and not a British one. And so, though golf may have become something like a world-wide epidemic, it was and radically remains a Scottish not British game. Burns, by the way, is not a British poet, nor was Harry Lauder a British comedian. And who in the whole wide world ever asked for a double 'British and soda'?

Who are they then, these people who refuse to be either English or British, but who inhabit the Northern end of the island of Britain (known to the world as England) and the many hundreds of islands off that Northern end? One of the many possible answers to that question is that they are about as confusing a collection of opposites as you are likely to meet anywhere in the world. They have more internal differences of character and opinion than almost any other nation. Yet each one of them is instantly recognizable as Scots, Scottish or Scotch—whatever term you prefer. For instance:

A dour, grim-faced, unemotional, inexpressive, unimaginative, mean, Puritanical materialist haunted by the sound of saxpences that go bang in the night. Such, I regret to say, is the image conjured up in many people's mind by the word Scotsman. A dreamy, proud, romantic, hopelessly unpractical kilted figure draped in tartan against a background of purple in inglorious technicolor and haunted by the sound of bogus Celtic music from fairyland. Such, I equally regret to say, is the image produced by the same word for many other people.

The only two qualities which the popular view allows these two contradictory characters of Scotsmen to possess are an inordinate love of whisky and the capacity for making fine fighting troops.

Neither of these two conceptions of the Scot is, of course, true; but there is just enough basis of truth in them to have been responsible for the legend. The basis of truth springs from the ancient difference between the Lowlander and the Highlander. And there still is enough of a difference between, let us say, the Gaelic-speaking Hebridean and the Lowland Aberdeenshire farmer to make the legend survive. But the truth is that nowadays the Scots blood is so mixed (look up the number of Highland names in the telephone book of any Lowland town) that most Scots somehow miraculously manage to combine something of the qualities of both these two types: it's all very confusing.

It's as confusing as is the racial origin of the Scots. Originally, about 1,500 years ago, they were Gaelic-speaking people who came over from Ireland and possessed all the knuckle-end of Britain we call Scotland today. To these were added other Celts of the Welsh speaking type in the South-West. Oh, by the way, never, never use the word Celt with a hard 'C' in Scotland. Kelt means a diseased salmon. Like the French with whom the Scots have so much in common (yes, they really do) they soften the 'C' in Celt. Then came Angles in the South-East, Scandinavians in the far North-East, Teutons and Flemings in the Middle East of the country. And to add the final exotic touch of garlic to the hotch-potch, the nearly four hundred years 'Auld Alliance' with France introduced a distinct French element.

The inquisitive traveller then who wants to understand the average Scot should remember that he is probably speaking to someone who contains in himself elements from all these sources. The most 'emotional' and imaginative Highlander will suddenly display the caution of some Lowland ancestor or the bone-headedness of a Scandinavian forebear. The most practical Lowland city business man may discover to you, after the third whisky, a passion for poetry. The most respectable home-loving, kirk-going elderly matron will surprise you by her love of France and her ability, after her own somewhat pedantic fashion, to speak the French language.

What combines all these different types who, in varying degrees, possess these opposing qualities? The first answer is the fact of Bannockburn. No, no, this is not a history lesson. But unless you understand that six and a half centuries ago an individual known as the 'Hammer of the Scots' (Edward I of England) hammered us not out of existence but into a hard intractable fact—which fact was subsequently established and confirmed at Bannockburn—you won't understand the Scots.

The second amongst many other possible answers (and oh, how I regret to have to say this!) is a kind of inferiority complex. Yes, this proud, gallant, warlike, sensitive, sometimes dour, sometimes gay people suffer from an inferiority complex which has been forced on them. It was forced on them when they as the smaller partner of a Union found themselves, in the eyes of the world, swallowed up by the larger partner; England.

That inferiority complex which has been troubling

us since the end of the 18th century onwards can manifest itself in many ways. The arrogant Scot who so loudly insists upon his nationality in England—but, be it noted, seldom on the Continent where he feels himself an equal; the pathetic tartan-tammied, whisky-swilling crowds who descend upon London for an International football match; the behaviour of so many Scottish Members of Parliament, and so on.

But let one obvious example speak for itself and then be done with the distasteful subject. When a distinguished English visitor is being welcomed at a public banquet in Scotland, how often, alas! do not the proceedings follow this form.

The chief welcomer rises and even before he begins to praise the visitor he announces with a smile that 'our guest of this evening has had the misfortune to be born on the wrong side of the Border' (laughter). He then goes on to make jokes about the 'provinciality of London' (more laughter). Finally, he welcomes the guest in due terms of praise. But he's got to go through this rigmarole first. It is a rigmarole to which the unfortunate Englishman has to respond by rising and saying with a smirk, 'As a mere Sassenach' (laughter). He then, if he can, proudly proclaims that he had a Scottish grandmother—or even worse, Grannie!

Those who doubt that all this is a sign of an inferiority complex are asked to think of the situation the other way round, to put the boot on the other foot. Imagine a distinguished Scot being welcomed at a banquet in London by the remark that the visitor was 'unfortunately born on the wrong side of the Border'. No Englishman or Londoner would dream of opening a speech in such a way: he is far too sure of himself.

But this inferiority complex (so largely and unfortunately so publicly manifested in the presence of the larger partner of the Union) disagreeable and embarrassing though it may be for us more travelled Scots who love our country, is not universal. It is moreover a small thing beside that real pride of race, that deep capacity for emotion, and be it added, endurance which are amongst the signs by which you may know, recognize and understand that confusing conglomeration of opposites, the Scot.

By what other qualities may you know him? By a maddening habit, if he is a certain type of Lowlander, of taking the simplest flight of fancy in words in which you may indulge literally—it is a Highlander who notes and admits this fact—by a complete incapacity, if he is a certain type of Highlander, to obey any time-table, or have any sense of time at all—it is a Highlander born and brought up in Edinburgh who states this—by an odd formality of manner and speech wholly foreign to the English mind, a formality which may sometimes appear laboured, and in another mood agreeably old-fashioned and civilized; by an incurable love of religious discussion and discursiveness, even if he be an atheist; by an excessive individuality, a love of 'hiving off' and doing things in his own way (they were a' oot o' step except oor Jock). And by many other things, the last and pleasantest of which is the truly staggering love of hospitality. This applies to the whole lot of them, Highlanders and Lowlanders alike, to every Scot alive.

Chapter Two

The Highlander and the Lowlander

The Highlander

IT has already been pointed out that the Highlanders and the Lowlanders have largely mixed their blood. But the difference in certain parts most distinctly does remain. If you are to understand the Scots you must understand this difference even as it exists today.

Here are two stories which I tell to illustrate some points I wish to make about that much misused, much sentimentalized-over figure, the Scottish Highlander.

Some time ago a Highland Lord Macdonald of the Isles, immensely proud and immensely impoverished, used, it is said, occasionally to visit London to attend the Lord Mayor's Banquet. He drove down to the English Capital in his own rather shabby coach. When he got to the heights of Finchley, however, he stopped and had one of his horses lightly shod with one gold shoe. The horse invariably cast this gold shoe just on the outskirts of the city. When someone asked Lord Macdonald the reason for this absurd extravagance, which he could ill afford, he said:

"I do it to let the citizens of London know that the Lord Macdonald of the Isles is come amongst their midst."

When he arrived at the Lord Mayor's Banquet one year he unfortunately found himself set very low at the table. A Cockney alderman twitted him on this and added that he would have thought after so long a journey Lord Macdonald would be nearer the head of the table. To which there came the classic reply:

"Where Lord Macdonald of the Isles sits *is* the head of the table."

The other story occurred during my own lifetime. Between the two wars there was a census of the population of the British Isles. With characteristic bureaucratic ineptitude some Government department sent to a certain Hebridean island a census-taking official from Whitehall to find out the ages of the people on the island—an official who could not speak Gaelic.

The poor man did his best, but what with the general uncertainty which the islanders themselves suffered from about their ages and the difficulty of the language, he found himself beat. He decided to call in help and visited one of the most prominent figures on the island, a local worthy whom (since many knew him) I shall just call MacX.

MacX was a splendid great figure of a man, large, tall, white-moustachioed, vigorous, strong, but with that soft gentle voice you get to perfection only in the West Highlands and Islands. MacX was a well-known figure to many sporting visitors to this island from all over the world, and his amiable habit of boasting about the qualities of his native island was well known. If you spoke of a particularly rare flower which grew only on the French Riviera, MacX would at once claim that only last year there had been plenty growing on the island.

The census official began by asking MacX whether in his opinion there were many octogenarians on the island. MacX's Gaelic was more fluent than his

English and the word 'octogenarian' was a bit of a facer for him, but he was not to be beat. "Octogenarians?" repeated once or twice in his soft and sighing voice, and then added, "Yess, yess, there wass two of them last year, but one of them flew away, and my brother shot the other one . . . Yess, yess, octogenarians, there wass two."

Now the point that emerges from this possibly apocryphal story about Lord Macdonald of the Isles and the undoubtedly true one about MacX is this. In each you get an example of the Highlander's capacity for combining pride with nimble wit and a touch of absurdity, even ridiculousness, which no one except a fellow Highlander can decide is deliberate or not.

Lord Macdonald was well aware that he could ill afford the loss of a golden shoe on each visit to London. He was well aware that most Londoners who met him just thought of him as an impoverished Northern nobleman. Yet his pride forced him to this extravagance, and his sense of humour as well as his *panache* made him explain it in the way he did. His nimble wit combined with pride and humour again in his brief reply to the Cockney alderman. He was well aware that the richer and slower-witted merchants of London would laugh at him for his pride, but he was damned well going to be proud and let everyone know it.

The worthy MacX may or may not have had an idea of what the pompous but bemused little Government official meant by the word 'octogenarians'. He may or may not have thought he was referring to a rare bird, but he was not going to let the opportunity slip of proudly boasting about his island and *possibly* in a consciously ridiculous or leg-pulling way.

If upon your visit to Scotland you travel to the far

North-West and to the islands you may not at first come across examples of this nimble-witted pride. The Highlanders of Scotland have suffered grievously from oppression and enforced emigration in the last two centuries, and there is an inescapable sadness in their race now which once was not there. (This is not too serious a book; and the present writer does not wish to dwell upon the deliberate destruction and driving out of his own folk. But it has to be mentioned.) You may, therefore, at first be impressed by their shyness and their withdrawal into themselves. But if you stay long and listen well enough you will hear some jewels of speech—as good as anything you will get in the West of Ireland.

I mention this quality in the Highlander because it is so far outside the usual popular conception of him. He is supposed to be romantic, dreamy, 'fey' (a shocking misuse of a Gaelic word meaning doomed) impractical yet brave. No doubt he is capable of displaying all these and other qualities. But at the same time he is a most amusing, quick-witted fellow with a strong sense of the ridiculous, and loves words for their own sakes. He will decorate any situation with words to make it picturesque even to the point of embarrassment.

When I was a very young man in lodgings in a Scottish town, my mother, who was then living in England, came up to visit me. I told my dear old Highland landlady, Mrs. R, that my mother would be coming to dinner, asked her to prepare a good one, and finally, and rather tentatively, suggested that she should put a curb upon her rather free tongue. "My mother is a lady who has lived much in England and may not understand all your jokes."

Mrs. R. was horrified. "There is nothing," she

exclaimed, "nothing that I would dare to say which would offend so fine a lady as the mother of a young gentleman like yourself, Mr. McLaren. No, no, have no fear. I will serve a good dinner and say nothing. I will be most tactful."

At the end of the meal my mother congratulated Mrs. R. on her cooking and also thanked her for looking after me so well and making me so comfortable. This set Mrs. R. off at once. She burst into a paeon of praise about my alleged good qualities and ended up by saying:

"Madam, it is a pleasure, a very great pleasure indeed, to look after a young gentleman like your son. Indeed I look after him as if he were my own son, indeed I do. Many is the time when he has come home late at night tired and perhaps a little bit gay and confused" (I saw what was coming but could not stop her) "many is the time that I have undressed him with these very hands and put him into bed in the same state of nature in which you brought him into the world, Madam."

This, I reflected, was dear Mrs. R.'s idea of being tactful! But there was no use in complaining. The Highland spate of words had been let free, and embarrassing or not, one had to put up with it.

THE BOGUS AND NOT SO BOGUS

This element in the Highland character is not much advertised in the popular writings about and manifestations of Scotland. Instead we draw to our visitors' attention other things, some of which are bogus, some half bogus, and some genuinely of the Highland character today, or rather such of it as is left in the denuded glens and islands of today.

The so-called 'Highland Games' organized on a grand scale and featured with much illustration in the glossy magazines are largely bogus. They are partly a relic of Victorian days when thoroughly denationalized chieftains liked to put on a romantic show *à la* Walter Scott novel for the benefit of visiting Royalty. They are partly nowadays also frankly commercial enterprises put on to boost the 'Come to Scotland' movement.

Your true Highlander is not a performing animal, and normally nowadays he does not wear the kilt. He is not without the spirit of competition, and no doubt he enters with a certain gusto into piping contests and some exhibitions of strength and skill. The whole open-air-music-hall atmosphere of these performances, however, is really foreign to his nature. And as for some of the contestants who come from the towns to perform at these games, the less said about them the better.

It is not the fault of those unfortunate little girls that they are dressed up in the essentially masculine (and this is an important point) garment of the kilt, that they are hung with clinking medals and made to dance masculine reels on open platforms. No, it is not their fault, but the imagination boggles and re-boggles at the thought of what Rob Roy, or any genuine old Highlander of the past, would say if he could see such exhibitions.

The wearing of that Highland garment the kilt as a masculine attire (that garment associated both romantically and on comic picture postcards with Scotsmen all over the world) is an example of something that was within living memory bogus, but is now rapidly becoming a genuine manifestation of Scottishness. How this has come about is not without interest. And if you are to understand the Scot and his present-day attitude to what is commonly thought of as his national garment, it is worth pausing to explain it.

The Wearing of the Kilt

When I was a small boy in Scotland in the first two decades of this century, the kilt was worn, the military apart, only by the following. (1) Highland lairds who, whether their names were Macdonald, Campbell, Brown, Jones, Robinson or Cohen, wished to establish the fact in the eyes of their neighbours by wearing 'the garb of old Gaul' that they had inherited or bought Scottish land. (2) Small boys of the upper-middle classes in big towns who on Sundays were dressed up in a preposterous combination of the kilt, a green jacket and an Eton collar! (3) Elderly cranks who for political or 'artistic' reasons wished to pretend that they were still living in the 18th century or earlier—or who were just professional romantics.

This absurd decline in the use of what had once been a graceful, useful and decorative Highland male garment had come about in this way. Until the rising under Prince Charles Edward Stuart of 1745 the kilt in one of its two forms (the great or small kilt) had been the normal attire of all Highland men. After the rising had been crushed, the London Government forbade 'the use of a distinctive Highland dress', and for over thirty years the Highland men had by law to wear breeks.

When, however, under the influence of the great Walter Scott, a romantic attitude towards the now

The kilt as worn on Sundays by small boys in
Good King Edward's reign

crushed and largely dispossessed Highlanders began to prevail, things changed. The kilt came back in the early years of the 19th century with a bang—but only as a snob garment. The final touch that made it fashionable in this kind was when George IV, upon his only visit to Scotland, draped his pudgy knees under a protective covering of pink tights in a kilt of what he was assured was the Royal Stuart tartan.

After that the Edinburgh tailors went to town over the kilt and the tartan in a big way. Every Highland gentleman, and many who liked to think of themselves as Highland gentlemen, promptly kilted themselves. The ordinary Scot, however, whether in the Highlands or Lowlands regarded this as a ridiculous affectation and would have nothing to do with it.

But the fashion did not die out. Under the great and benevolent Queen Victoria, who sincerely loved Scotland, it continued to flourish in certain circles. She dressed up her husband, the Prince Consort, in a kilt when he came to Braemar. She dressed up her sons and German nephews in the kilt. She even (and one suspects to their embarrassment) succeeded in getting some of her ghillies and Highland servants to wear it.

The Victorian tradition lasted until 1914, and indeed till a few years later. And so it was that until the 1920s the kilt was worn only as a snob badge to proclaim the proprietorship of land, or by small boys as a Sunday-go-to-meeting dress, or by cranks.

Today all that is changed. It would be safe to say that it would be impossible for any visitor to Scotland, especially in the summer and holiday months, to travel anywhere, town or country, without seeing many perfectly ordinary and unclass-conscious Scottish males wearing the kilt. They wear it, be it admitted, in varying degrees of gracefulness or uncouthness; but they do wear it and are not conspicuous for doing so.

What had happened was that between the two wars the young people of the Scottish towns, as did the young people all over the rest of Britain, discovered the countryside and their right to enjoy it. They discovered something else at the same time; that there existed a national garment which was decorative, useful and comfortable for wearing in the open air, and which was, like the well-known advertisement for the London Underground, 'cool in Summer, warm in Winter'—the kilt.

The result was that the countryside soon began to swarm with young hikers, campers, walkers, anglers, mountaineers and so on, all adding colour to our scene by wearing the kilt. Later on, and especially today, this coincided with the so-called form of emancipation for young women which allowed them to wear trousers. In modern Scotland then you often have the somewhat comical spectacle of a large group of young people composed of youths wearing the skirted garment of the kilt and the girls wearing the breeks! Whether this has any psychological effect on the growing dominance of the female sex is uncertain.

Finally, since so many thousands of young people of all classes from the cities, towns and countryside were wearing the kilt, certain middle-aged people, who would never have dreamed of doing such a thing before, also took to the kilt. And so you have even certain business men with Scottish consciousness about them wearing the kilt as an evening attire, and sometimes even in the daytime and at their offices.

The Right to Wear a Tartan

With all this popularity of the kilt, the grand old hackneyed problem of 'What tartan have I the right to wear?' began to raise its pedantic head. Let me cut to the heart of this problem, which isn't really a problem at all, by telling you, especially if you are a visitor to Scotland, that you have the right to wear any tartan that tickles your fancy. Of course, if your name happens to be Macdonald or Campbell, or if you have any relationship with these two great clans it would be in a sense fitting, if you want to wear the tartan, to sport the red one *associated* with the Macdonalds or the green with the Campbells. If you are called after one of the many smaller clans (no names, no tartan-drill) and if you like the tartan that the tailors of the romantic period in Scottish literature invented for you, by all means wear it. If, on the other hand, another one pleases you better, choose it *simply because you like it*, and no one can say you nay.

All this complicated talk of surnames which you will sometimes see stuck up in Scottish tailoring or fancy goods shops telling you what names are associated with what tartans is so much ballyhoo, amiable ballyhoo, but ballyhoo none the less. The name Johnson is supposed to indicate that the bearer belongs to a sept (a misuse of the word for dependent clan) of the Macdonalds. One wonders what Dr. Samuel Johnson would have said to such a fantastic notion! If he had ever been induced to wear a tartan garment and had sported a Macdonald waistcoat it would have been because he had met Flora Macdonald on his Tour to the Hebrides, or because he liked the look of it, not because his name came from a dependant clan.

But the notion is too fantastic even to contemplate.

So, if you do like the look of a tartan and want to wear a tie or a waistcoat or a shirt composed of it, go ahead and wear it and choose one which you like. Pay no attention to any Scottish pedant who asks you if you have a grandmother who was a Macdonald or a Stewart or a Macgregor. You will usually find that those who are keen on such genealogical rights to wear a particular combination of coloured cloths known as a tartan do not possess Highland names themselves. They merely seek to justify the fact that they are wearing a particular 'sett' by digging up some mythical Highland grandmother of their own.

I don't want to leave the impression, however, that the tartan and above all the revival of the wearing of the kilt in modern Scotland is what is known as a 'racket' or even a temporary fashion. Tartan was for over a thousand years the cloth worn by Highland folk. For something like the same period, something approximating to the modern kilt was worn by Highland men. Nowadays nearly all Scotland, Lowland as well as Highland, has revived the tartan and, to a certain extent, the kilt. It is an authentically Scottish tradition (even if it was purely Highland in origin) now come authentically back into use. The only thing that is bogus, or, more charitably, semi-bogus, is the rigid association of certain tartans with certain names.

A Genuine, Non-Bogus Highland Tradition

The most genuine Highland tradition that remains is, of course, the Highland language of Gaelic. It is, and one admits this with regret, fighting a losing battle. Nevertheless, at the risk of offending some of my Irish friends, I state that it is a more genuine tradition than is the Irish Gaelic in Ireland. There has, of course, been no attempt to force it on the population as an official language. But it does exist, and as a very precious heritage, in the Highlands of the West and in the Hebrides. More than anything else enforced emigration was the enemy of the Scottish Gaelic in Scotland. Thus you get the partly absurd, partly sad, fact that there are considerably more native Gaelic-speakers, the descendants of emigrants, in Nova Scotia than in Scotland.

Of course, the Gaelic language is not being allowed to die out, if ever it does die out, without a struggle. A vigorous and nation-wide society (I will not trouble the English-speaking reader with its Gaelic name) exists for the fostering of the language and incidentally the music associated with the language. It is a gallant society, and it has helped many people to preserve the language of their forefathers, and others to learn it afresh. But alas! what can it do in the face of the radio and the cinema which between them are plugging every Highland child's ears with English and American.

Real and admirable though the tradition of the Gaelic language is in Scotland, it like everything else attracts the bogus and the second-rate. It would be difficult to think of a more delightful and natural party than a true Gaelic *Ceilidh*—an informal gathering to sing songs and tell stories—in the Outer Isles. Alas! the organized Ceilidh (the very phrase is a contradiction in terms) as often held in the towns is an embarrassing parody of the real thing. The visitor to Scotland is warmly recommended to accept an invitation to a *Ceilidh* in the Highlands or Islands if it is given by word of mouth. He is cautioned against attending any 'advertised *Ceilidh*' in Edinburgh, Glasgow or anywhere else. It will almost certainly be as bogus Highland as was the spectacle of poor George IV in a kilt in Edinburgh—pink tights and all!

And so the Highlanders, the real Gaels of Scotland, though much reduced in numbers, continue to exist as a lively and enlivening element in the Scottish scene. It is the Highland heritage that Scotland still puts most prominently into the shop window devoted to Scottish tradition. The bagpipes, the kilt, the tartan, the Celtic fluency of speech—you may find all these and other Gaelic things all over Scotland, but their origin was in the Highlands. Scotland would indeed be a dull country if you removed from it all the few genuine pure Gaels left in the Highlands and Islands. Without the Highland traditions and heritage, however, even as they exist in the Lowlands and in the great towns Scotland would just not be Scotland; it would be unthinkable.

The Lowlander

The Lowlanders have suffered almost as much as have the Highlanders from sentimental fiction and, of course, in what one might call 'Music-Hall', or 'comic postcard' misrepresentation. It is on the unfortunate Lowlander's character that are based all the 'Scotch stories' about meanness, caution and taciturnity. Since I have told two stories about the Highlander in a slightly comic *rôle* I feel entitled to venture on one about the Lowlander. More than any other that I know it epitomises the Lowlander's cautious and taciturn fear of 'giving himself away' by enthusiasm.

A Lowland Story

A newly-married young couple of my acquaintance had returned from their honeymoon which they had spent on some Mediterranean island of great beauty. They had taken a number of photographs of the most celebrated 'beauty spots' of this island in order to keep memories of the circumstances of their newly-wedded bliss. These photographs they pasted into an album. And when they came back to Scotland they showed the volume to an elderly uncle of the young woman. This old gentleman was an amiable and, at heart, kindly man; he was also an Aberdeenshire farmer of the purest Lowland blood. Behind him there were generations of other Aberdeenshire farmers who, though they may have been generous in other things, never gave themselves away in speech.

The old man took the album and slowly looked through it without speaking a word. Having reached the end, with equal slowness, he turned the pages back again. The young couple, a trifle dampened by his silence, awaited his verdict. At length it came. Putting a broad spatulate finger upon one picture he uttered the words "That's the worst."

In fairness it should be added that a little later on when the same Aberdeenshire uncle had had time to reflect and re-inspect the album he may well have ventured on some careful praise. But the point is that before he said anything else he had to make it crystal clear that his eagle, and would-be unenthusiastic eye, had detected the particular picture that was the least successful.

Any artist, in particular any writer, who earns his living in Scotland is well accustomed and hardened to this Lowland habit of preliminary denigration before any other criticism is offered. He may have spent years in writing a book, and his Scottish Lowland friend, having most carefully read it, may have enjoyed it with genuine appreciation. Before that appreciation is expressed, however, the writer must be prepared for some such opening remark as: "It's a pity you made that mistake about the misplaced comma on page 22." Nevertheless, having endured that opening gambit of niggling dispraise, the author may be assured that, if he cares to listen, he will receive real appreciative if not exactly lyrical criticism of his work.

Meanness about Money

I feel a certain meanness myself in including such a subject under the Lowland heading, for the Lowlander is by no means meaner than the Highlander, and can often, with less ostentation, be more deeply generous. However, it is with the Lowland temperament as, superficially experienced by the foreigner, that this world-wide reputation of the Scot is associated. So here goes:

The reputation is indeed world-wide. You have to be a Scot, and a travelled Scot, to realize this. Wherever you go in America, in the Dominions, in Europe (with the exception of one country which I shall shortly mention) if you announce your nationality as Scottish you will instantly be greeted (possibly with the idea of making you feel at home) with a succession of comic stories about your compatriots' meanness. After that there may be pleasant stories about Scottish hospitality or even 'romantic reflection' on Scotland's past. The immediate result of the mention of Scotland and the

Scots, however, is to provoke thoughts of meanness in money.

This reputation has its origin as far back as 1603 when our King James VI came down to London to be King James I of England. He brought with him in his train a crowd of impoverished Scottish nobles who had to try and keep a style befitting their ancient lineage on what were in London contemptibly small incomes. Their pride and their poverty combined to give them an air of aloof and ridiculous stinginess. Later, when in 1707 the Union of Parliaments took place, the nobles were joined by many other humbler and compatriot place-seekers. These too in their own sphere of life were commensurately impoverished but were equally proud. The reputation of Scotch meanness then in London in the early 18th century got a fresh lease of life.

With the increasing prosperity of Scotland later on in the 19th century the legend might have died a natural death and have been forgotten had it not been for a particular class of our own community—the 'Scotch comedian'. Of course there had been jokes in *Punch* and other comic journals in London for many years on Scotch meanness, but far more important to the spreading of the legend than these was the genius of the late Sir Harry Lauder.

Lauder was in his own way undoubtedly a genius. The late James Agate, the dramatic critic, used to say that there were only two stage personalities whom he had ever seen who made themselves felt *through* the curtain, before it went up. These two were Sarah Bernhardt and Harry Lauder. Lauder sang his way round the English speaking world, and indeed such was the power of his stage personality that he was partly appreciated even by audiences who had very little knowledge of English—still less of Scots! Wherever he sang, the prime joke in his stock in trade of humour was, of course, Scotch stinginess. Though capable of acts of anonymous and considerable generosity on the quiet, he even 'put on an act' of meanness in his personal life so as to support the stage character he nightly assumed.

A whole host of lesser Scotch comedians followed and imitated Lauder. These in their turn were followed by the designers of comic Scotch postcards and by other professional humorists. The funny story about Scotch stinginess was now thoroughly and probably permanently launched, and was received with relish in every country in the world, with one exception.

That exception which I mentioned earlier is France. This is not because the French are not conscious of the Scots. Indeed there is no country in Europe where, on his nationality alone, the Scot is more welcome than in France. It would be too much to claim that the French like the Scots too well to propagate a legend about them. The probable reason is that the French themselves have such a reputation for meanness that they have a fellow feeling for us. In short, they don't think caution about money matters a funny trait. They've got too much of it themselves.

Is the Legend about Meanness True?

Yes, in one sense it is true, in another most certainly not. The Scot does tend to be more careful of his pence than does the Englishman. On the other hand, he frequently startles not only the English but other of his neighbours by being reckless with his pounds. This apparent contradiction is based on his history.

Scotland has until quite recent times been, in material things, a very poor country. For centuries the Scot has had to struggle to make a living at all. And be it noted, this struggle was hardest in the Lowland districts and Border districts where the weather has always been harsh, the land, until treated by modern methods, unrewarding, and, in the old days, the possibility of savage warfare from the invaders across the Border always present. In order merely to keep alive, the Scot until not long ago simply had to mind each penny that passed through his hands.

On the other hand he has always been adventurous. The fact that you will find travelled Scots in any remote corner of the earth to which you may go proves this. In order to satisfy his sense of adventure then he will not risk his pence; but he will frequently, and most recklessly, risk his pounds. The Darien scheme when half Scotland, including thousands of 'sober, cautious, Lowland' business men, ruined herself for the visionary idea of a Scottish colony, is one example. The rising of 1745 for the Stuarts under Prince Charles Edward (I suppose I have to call him 'Bonnie Prince Charlie'!) is another. Not only the celebrated Highlanders, but many Lowland men of position and property, risked and lost all their material possessions in this venture, which seemed to most Englishmen of the time, even Jacobite Englishmen, sheer folly.

There are plenty of examples to prove this 'pound-folly' of the Scots, but there are not many 'stories' about it. Stories about his stinginess are, of course, legion. Everyone has his own favourite. Mine is the one about the old keen Scots golfer who was seen leaning gloomily over the rail which surrounds the last green at St. Andrews. For weeks he had been occupied in the lugubrious pastime of just watching other people play on the most famous golf course in the world.

"Why are you no' playing, Sandie?" someone asked him.

"I've lost my ball" was the laconic but heartbreaking reply.

There is another tale which pleases me, but I cannot make up my mind whether it is an illustration more of Scots stinginess, or Scots pride—or at least Scots hardiness.

Two Scots were coming home on a darkened night. One of them bore in his pocket the precious cargo of a full whisky bottle. He slipped on the frosty pavement and fell severely, striking his head on the hard stone. As he lay half-stunned upon the ground he could feel moisture. He dipped his finger in it and put it to his tongue. He then uttered the classic remark (and I apologise to those who have heard it before) "Thank God it's only blood."

And so, borne on the flood of stories, as good as, worse, or possibly better than these two I have quoted, the partly-true legend of 'Scotch meanness' goes merrily on. Possibly the strongest element in the Scottish nature to contradict it, or at least the one most obvious to visitors, is the Scots love of giving hospitality. This is truly prodigal, but will be dealt with in a later chapter. How often, however, does one not hear a Scotch-meanness story capped by the teller with some half-apologetic admission such as, "But, my goodness, they are a hospitable people. When I was in Scotland last year . . . "

The Other and Better Side of the Penny

Taciturnity, fear of giving oneself away, meanness

in money! This is indeed an unflattering list of qualities for anyone of Highland blood and name to attribute to his Lowland compatriots. Let amends then be made at once, and the best way is simply to mention two names and one tradition. The names are those of Robert Burns and Walter Scott; the tradition is that of the 'Border Ballads'.

No two men were more generous of *themselves*, gave themselves more freely away than Burns and Scott. Each of them was all heart; and through their differing forms of genius and talent and intellect they gave of those two hearts most prodigally to all the world.

For once the *cliché* 'to all the world' is justified. The poetry of Burns is known in every country in Europe and America, and even in some Asiatic lands. Whether you are moved by Burns's poetry or not, you cannot have avoided somewhere at some time singing or mumbling a few lines from his 'Auld Lang Syne'—English readers are implored to remember that 'syne' begins with an S and not a Z—and the song has at some time been sung in every, literally every, country in the world.

Scott's novels may or may not be much read now—though it is remarkable to note the enthusiasm some of them still arouse—but there can hardly be any other imaginative writer of fiction who more widely and deeply influenced the world than did Walter Scott. The Romantic Movement may have originated in the minds of other and profounder poets, playwrights, essayists and writers in England, Germany and France, but it was Walter Scott who spread its fame and what might be called the fact of it all over the world. His novels were in the days of long before our present 'mass communication' translated into nearly every European language as soon as they appeared from the printing presses in Edinburgh. When, by means of the stage coach, news of his death reached Petrograd, a period of official mourning was ordained at the Imperial Court of the 'Czar of all the Russias'.

Both the peasant-farmer Robert Burns from Ayrshire and the gentleman's son Walter Scott (related to the great family of the Scotts of Harden) from the Borders were Lowlanders of the Lowlanders, in their blood, bones, sinews and (and this is important) in their hearts. The difference between them and most of their other fellow Lowland Scots was that they were able to express what was in their hearts. They were enabled to do this partly, of course, by the impelling power of genius, and also partly by the fact that they did not suffer from the inhibiting fear of *appearing* to be emotional which afflicts so many of their compatriots. They gave themselves away; and how rich was the gift that they gave to the world.

Because these two Lowland Scots of genius were able to express themselves and just because they were unusual but by no means unique in this respect, it should not be supposed that they were unScottish in their temperaments. The exact opposite is the truth. In giving themselves away they also gave something from the heart of Lowland Scotland to the world. That something was the gift of lyricism and the quality of romance.

Other and nameless or at least forgotten Lowland Scots gave the same qualities to the world before them. The Border Ballads, though not known outside the small countryside of their origin (i.e. the land just north of the line between England and Scotland) until less than 200 years ago have now joined the body of the great poetry which has come out of Europe.

We do not know who were the authors of these anonymous ballad poems save that they were ancestors of the men who today inhabit the Border hills and who still speak much of the same language as that of the ballads. When we hear an old Border farmer or shepherd talking today amongst his own folk we know that his accents are those of the ballad-makers of long ago. His laconic and matter-of-fact statements may give no hint of the feeling and the capacity for romance that is in him, but it is there. It was expressed by his forefathers in apparently simple verse whose strange and thrilling magic has caught the ear of the world.

The truth is that underneath the often assumed taciturnity and fear of 'giving himself away' the average Lowland Scot is an emotional and romantic individual. When his temperament is informed with genius or sometimes no more than with talent, he is able to express this side of his nature. When he is denied this outlet he may seem to the outside world to be even more taciturn than ever, but the capacity for emotion and for romantic feeling is there nonetheless.

Sometimes it breaks out in embarrassing sentimentality or, in that well-known (and, in theatrical circles at one time, highly saleable commodity) Celtic whimsy. This can to the native Scot of any taste be even more embarrassing than sentimentality. The visitor to Scotland, however, is unlikely to see much evidence of this sentimentality or whimsy. It is usually kept for export, or indulged in by expatriates who have rubbed off some of their taciturnity, but have not the talent nor the use to express their feelings properly.

Extremes Meet

The purest repository of the Scottish Highland tradition is now to be found in the Outer Hebridean Islands. The strongest outpost of the old Lowland ways in speech and manner is Aberdeenshire and generally in Buchan, that hump of the mainland of Scotland which sticks out eastward into the North Sea just south of the Moray Firth.

In a Hebridean island such as Barra, the setting for 'Whisky Galore', Gaelic is the main language of all the natives, and until recently there were a few monoglots or at least those who were unfamiliar with English. The Barra men may have to work hard for a living but they give an impression of taking life easily. "When God made time He made plenty of it" is a favourite saying of these people who are gay, witty, amusing, or sometimes melancholy, but never inhibited. They are naturally poetic, musical and perhaps impractical. They are amongst the most delightful people you could meet anywhere, and you can make friends with them at once.

In Aberdeenshire the folk there still speak without affectation the broad old Lowland Scots tongue which can to a visiting Englishman be almost as incomprehensible as is the Gaelic. They too work hard for their living by the land and from the sea, but they are highly practical; and time means money to them. They are full of the Lowland virtues and failings which have been described above.

What is it then that joins these peoples, different in race, language and temperament? Where do these extremes within Scotland meet? Sometimes it is in Religion. The Outer Islands are in parts the strongholds of the extremest forms of Presbyterianism. This also you will find in Aberdeenshire. On many of the Outer Isles there are indigenous Highland Catholics who have kept the 'old Faith' undisturbed by the Reformation. There are also Aberdeenshire Catholics who have done the same. Sometimes it is the heritage of the land and seas around it which links these farming and fishing folk. Sometimes maybe it is other qualities in them which it is easier for a foreigner than for one of their own compatriots to perceive.

In general, however, the strongest link between the Gaelic speaking Islander and the Aberdeenshire or Border farmer is quite simply the fact of nationality. When the lad from the Islands goes to do his National Service and meets another of his own age in the same army unit or in the same ship he recognizes him as a compatriot; and though may not agree with him, or may even fight and quarrel with him, he *feels* a bond with him. It is the same with their elders and in other walks of life. Business, adventure, the pursuit of knowledge, or one of a hundred other reasons, may have taken them abroad. But anywhere overseas, or for that matter across the Border, your Highlander and your Lowlander will feel themselves to be Scotsmen first and last; only after that will they recognize their differences.

Despite the Union of Crowns in 1603, despite the merging of the Governments of the two countries of England and Scotland in the Union of Parliaments in 1707, the old Kingdom of Scotland unites its sons despite all their differences. The fact of nationality is stronger than the power of any statute; it can even unite a Highlander and a Lowlander.

Having written that sentence, which I had intended to be the last in this chapter, I am reminded that one of the best, light-hearted and sympathetic appraisals of the Highland character I have read came from a Lowland pen.

"The Highlander is a strange, if likable, fellow. He has often been described by his critics as feckless and slothful, which is just another way of saying that he happens to like doing things in his own way and in his own time. He often considers that the art of living is more important than the cost of living, and he has an incurable habit of being civilised.

"Highlanders haven't quite cottoned on to the idea that low pressure enjoyment is no longer fashionable and that you can't get far without a time and motion approach. Highlanders tend to be passionate in a restful kind of way, and that is why presumably there has not been a great influx of lawyers, the harbingers of progress, north of the Grampians.

"The fact must be faced, however, that it is very hard for a Lowlander to get really in cahoots with a Highlander. There is a psychological as well as a geographical Highland line. Highlanders either resist the idea of Lowlanders getting to know them too well or they genuinely believe that it is impossible.

"More than once we have suggested to a Highlander that the best way to lick the Highlands economically into shape is to let the Lowlanders in to do some Klondyking. Lowlanders tend to be eager beavers, and they could tackle the rough work in the Highlands while allowing the Highlanders themselves to look after the loftier things. This, we honestly think, would be an ideal compromise.

"No Highlander we have met will accept this idea. It offends his conception of the clan spirit or arouses other mysterious resentments. He is apt to fly into a dark and gentlemanly passion if you put up this proposition to him. He has his own logic which has nothing to do with the syllogism. If your name doesn't begin with 'Mac' you can only go so far with a Highlander and no further. Scratch him and you find a Liberal or something equally strange. The Highland problem is really a problem in semantics.

"We remember hearing a story about how a party of students from the South who had been camping near a Highland village had enjoyed themselves so much that they decided to show their gratitude. They looked around and found a field which was uncommonly full of stones. So they set about removing the stones.

"They worked from dawn to sunset taking the stones away from the field, and, as they toiled, a number of Highlanders watched them from the road, puffing at their pipes, and occasionally making observations such as: 'Are they not enchoying themselves, the young chentlemen? Chust watch how the stones are flying from their hands, like pirds.' Well eventually the field was cleared of stones and the young workers, exhausted, staggered from their work.

"As they filed past him the oldest Highlander stopped the leader and said: 'It was a great sight, to see you chentlemen working so hard on this fine day, taking all these stones away from the field. It has given us great pleasure to watch you. Very great pleasure.' The leader looked gratified. 'Tell me,' asked the old man, 'will you be putting them back again tomorrow for we should not like to miss the sight. It would give us great pleasure. Very great pleasure.' "

Those paragraphs came from the 'Scotsman's Log', a daily causerie in *The Scotsman*, and were written by Mr. J. W. Taylor, a Lowlander if ever there was one.

As a Scottish writer of Highland origin, I pay tribute to them; I certainly could not better them. Yes, there are some Lowlanders who can not only write on the Highlanders in a sense of nationality, but can understand them.

Chapter Three

The Pleasures and Civilities

Love

A PARISIAN lady of the 'half-world' in the 1920s once gave it as her opinion that 'Scotsmen must be amongst the best lovers in Europe'. This statement seemed to the present writer (who was then living in Paris pretending to be a student) so staggering, even preposterous, that his curiosity prompted him to gain from a friend of his an introduction to this light-hearted lady. He went further, he pressed her for her reasons for her remarkably flattering judgement on his fellow countrymen.

No, so it appeared, she had not had much experience of love with Scotsmen—one, two, possibly even three, but she could not be certain. No, she was judging merely by the appearance of Scotsmen. The appearance! This sounded even more puzzling; but she explained herself. She had seen many Scottish troops of all ranks during the first World War and had been immensely impressed by the virility of their outward show. She expatiated enthusiastically, very Frenchly and very femininely on the proud upright bearing of these stocky little men with thin waists and kilted behinds that stuck out like the tail feathers of a barnyard cock. "They must be real men," she said.

One sees what she meant, for Scotsmen in matters of

love are naturally very virile and it is not too fanciful to suppose that one may see something of the outward and visible sign of that virility in the pouting swagger of a kilted figure in uniform. But alas! having admitted Scottish virility and the possibility of its showing itself in the male form and style in 'the Garb of Old Gaul', there the matter ends. To be what the lady described as 'amongst the best lovers in Europe' one needs more than virility, one needs the display of enthusiasm not only for the lady one is loving, but for love itself. One needs also a certain refinement of delight in the way that enthusiasm is expressed. No one could claim such qualities for the average Scottish male, no matter how amorous he might be.

'Simplicity', as Wilde said, 'is the last refuge of the complex'. And it might well be that a Parisian light lady of love, grown tired of the refined manners, mannerisms and posturings of her more accomplished swains, would relish the direct approach of the average Scottish male. But this is a small foundation on which to base the statement that 'Scotsmen must be amongst the best lovers in the world'. They have their qualities, but they are not that.

They are, on the whole, less (I will not say hypocritical) but less evasive about sex than are the Englishmen. They either don't want it even in the form of social intercourse and make it abundantly plain by showing that they do not like the society of women or they want it very much and pursue their object directly. They don't talk about it much. The long and boringly told salacious story which is so tiresome a feature of Anglo-Saxon male club life (and which is, of course, indicative of a suppressed interest) is, naturally, not unknown in Scottish male society. I do not think, however, that it is boasting to indulge in the generalization that it is less prevalent.

The avoidance of female society by the men when they are not immediately and actively interested in them is in Scotland, one regrets to say, very prevalent. It manifests itself in all classes of Scottish society, amongst the civilized well-off professional men in the Capital and amongst the simpler and remoter country folk from the farms. At a gathering in one of the larger drawing-rooms of the noble New Town of Edinburgh you will see the men congregating at one end of the room, leaving the women (and how enchanting Scotswomen can be) to their own devices at the other. Yes, this is much worse in Scotland than in England. I used to think that the uncivilized British habit of shooing the women out of the room immediately at the end of dinner and not rejoining them until it is time for the party to break up, did not originate in 18th and 19th century England. But now I wonder.

The voluntary segregation of the sexes during social occasions can be pushed to a ludicrous extent at country or village-hall dances. I remember attending one of these functions in the farming district of the far North-East. When I came in I noticed all the men and the village lads lined up along one wall of the room. Along the opposite wall there sat or stood a collection of as sonsie lassies as I have ever seen. The girls chatted away amongst each other with animation and occasionally looked across the room at the men, with whom presumably they were going to dance. The men either said nothing or appeared to be absorbed in farming talk. 'How long', I asked myself, 'is this going to go on?'

I was answered by the appearance of a beribboned

Master of Ceremonies who stood up at the end of the room, signalled to the band to strike up the opening chord of a dance, and then bellowed out "Tak your partners". The effect was immediate.

The line of men and the line of lassies hurled themselves across the room like two waves of the sea. One could almost hear the shock of their meeting. Then to the thud and beat of perfect time, each couple swung splendidly into some old-fashioned Scottish country dance They danced magnificently; it was exhilarating even to watch them. 'Now', I said to myself, 'the ice is broken'. But it wasn't. The moment the band ceased to play, each man did not so much release his partner as appear to reject her. He then rejoined his associates on the male side of the room.

It would be wrong to leave the impression that Scotsmen in all their relationships with their womenfolk are no more than virile oafs. Scotsmen can make excellent husbands, splendid sons to their mothers and *sometimes* appealing sweethearts. When they do, on rare occasions, become vocal on the theme of love they can be eloquently vocal. After all, some of the most moving love-poetry in these islands has been composed in the Scottish tongue or by Scotsmen writing in English. Burns's 'Ae Fond Kiss' is in its sad, sensuous Scottish way as exquisite as is Shakespeare's 'Oh Mistress Mine' in its more triumphant manner. But then Scottish love-poetry is yet one more example of the capacity for paradox, for the unexpected combination of opposites in the Scottish character.

Most of these generalizations about the Scottish male's attitude towards women apply to the Highlander as well as to the Lowlander—but not quite. When your Highlander is a native Gaelic speaker he starts, as far

There are 20 ways of telling a girl you love her in
Gaelic without using the same word twice

as the power to express his emotion is concerned, with a distinct advantage over his Lowland or Scots-speaking compatriot. Nor is this all a matter of the Gaelic temperament; it is also linguistic. There are twenty different ways of telling a girl that you love her in the Gaelic language without ever using the same word twice.

This rush of amorous Gaelic words to the uninhibited Highlandman's head must be an intoxicating experience for him. To a girl, susceptible to flattery, it must too, at first, be delightful. As in Ireland, however, the Celtic male is sometimes inclined to exhaust and satisfy his passion in mere eloquence. Not a very satisfactory state of affairs for either the lover or the beloved! For all the perils that must have lain in frequenting his society, most women would prefer the Lowland practical (and eloquent) Robert Burns.

So far I have spoken only about the Scots male's attitude towards love and sex. It really would be an impertinence for me to generalize at any length about my female compatriots on this theme. This, however, can safely be said. The average decent Scotswoman is in this matter more like her opposite number in France than in England. She is, like the Frenchwoman, in all that concerns love and marriage eminently practical. She is, of course, capable of romance and deep feeling, but as in France when it comes to the important business of choosing a mate and building a home she seldom makes the mistake of letting her heart rule her head.

When, poor lass, she goes to the bad, she goes very bad indeed and (and here, of course, she differs from the Frenchwoman) without grace or style. Maybe it is some heritage of Puritanism that makes it so, but there can be few drabber drabs in Europe than the 'unfortunates' of Edinburgh, Glasgow and the bigger Scottish cities.

While on the subject of love and marriage, a word must be said about the youthful age at which boys and girls are allowed in Scotland to contract a civil marriage. Bastardy, though fortunately less frequent now, used in the days of Scotland's rural poverty to be very prevalent. Scots law detests bastardy and has from before the Reformation and afterwards endeavoured to fight it.

To this end it fixes the marriageable age without the consent of parents at sixteen, and until fairly recent times made marriage by declaration before witnesses an easy affair to contract. Whether Scots law is right in regarding the creation of a large number of illegitimate children as a greater evil than those that may spring from easily and youthfully contracted marriages is a matter of opinion on which most Scots and English people differ. It is, however, very unlikely that Scots law in the foreseeable future will change.

It is likely then that for some time those sometimes romantic but more frequently foolish or disastrous dashes across the Border by young English couples will continue. Maybe some more stringent law about the length of time of 'residence' in Scotland will be introduced. This would help matters in regard to runaway couples. But for Scots young people the law will almost certainly remain the same.

The Pleasures of the Table—Food

In the matter of food we have once more an example

of the contradictions that lie within the Scottish character. Celtic peoples are, as anyone who knows the beloved land of Ireland can testify, not good cooks; they do not care much for the pleasures of the table. Scotland is by no means all Celtic in blood or tradition, and she does not by any means inherit all over the country this unfortunate Gaelic tradition. Indeed in the past she had something of an international reputation for her *cuisine*. It may not have been to everyone's tastes, but it was distinctive, and the Scots were consciously proud of it. Before dealing with what remains of this tradition, let the worst be got out of the way by dealing with the average Scotsman's attitude to the pleasures of the table today.

It is (and it is with shame that one admits this) almost non-existent. Since the Industrial Revolution and the creation of the large cities, counted head by head the average Scot hardly cares what he eats at all. Or if he is selective it is only to dislike and reject any refined or delicate form of cooking. The food offered in the *average* (I italicize and repeat that word partly out of a desire to be fair, and partly to protect myself) the average public eating place in Scotland is lamentable. It is dull, overcooked, tasteless and presented completely without imagination. English gastronomes are always complaining about the food in the public eating places of their country. If they want to know what can be done to make good food almost uneatable save by the very hungry, they should come to Scotland or go to Ireland.

AND YET how superb good Scottish food, cooked and presented in the traditional way, can be! You may have eaten fish all over the world but you will never enjoy one more than a freshly-caught herring from the

North Sea or the Atlantic cooked in the Scottish way, split open and with oatmeal. Not far behind is the Scottish brown trout caught from running water and presented in the same way. The haggis, that source of so much music-hall and cartoonists' humour, when properly made by a good butcher and well-cooked is a fine savoury and satisfying dish. Forfar bridies (a delicious savoury meat pancake), Scotch strawberries (the largest in Europe), Scotch mutton and beef, really good Scotch broth, other soups, the cakes, the sweet dishes, even the humble turnips prepared and cooked in the Scottish manner, and so on . . . the mouth of him who holds this pen waters merely to set such things down.

The truth is the material for our Scottish tables is magnificent. All over Scotland you will find places where it is cooked and presented simply and traditionally; and when you find it you could scarcely wish to fare better. Alas! you have to look for such places. The modern town-inhabiting Scot has vitiated his palate and has turned his back upon the excellent traditions of the Scottish cuisine.

When I mention the traditions I am thinking of the descriptions of some 18th century or early 19th century meals of which I have read. These traditions do survive here and there, but mostly in private houses—and in the country. Also, when one talks about the traditions of Scottish cookery, one should remember that, even on this poor country in the past, the French influence was at work for centuries. The modern Scottish housewife still asks her butcher for a 'gigot' of mutton. She calls the dish on which it is served an ashet (*assiette*); and the haggis itself derives from *hachis* or minced meat.

Drink

To understand the Scottish attitude towards drink you must again recall the contradictions in his nature. Scotland as a Northern country much afflicted in the long winter by vile weather has produced a superb protection against it in the best whisky in the world. At the same time one should not forget that for centuries, and long after the 'Auld Alliance' with France had become only a sentimental memory more claret per head was drunk in Scotland than in any other country in Europe.

We were only slowly prevented from drinking it in the large quantities which we once used to absorb when, as a result of the Union we had to take the wine of England's 'oldest ally' Portugal.

> "*Firm and erect the Caledonian stood;*
> *Old was his mutton, and his claret good*
> *Let him drink port the Saxon cried.*
> *He drank the poison and his spirit died.*"

So wrote Home, the author of *Douglas, A Tragedy* in the latter half of the 18th century. I am happy to report that claret is still the most popular wine in Scotland amongst those who have any feeling for tradition.

But these two traditions,the whisky-drinking tradition and the by no means yet moribund claret and wine-drinking tradition are not so much at war with each other, but exist uneasily together. They exist sometimes in the same individual. You will find a man in Scotland in a mood which may last for months abjuring his native spirit and sticking to claret. Then suddenly, as if almost impelled by the lash of winter, he will return to whisky.

So far I have spoken about the more estimable, or at

least less reprehensible drinking habits of the Scot. As all the world knows, he has acquired something of a reputation on this reprehensible side. This reputation springs not so much from alcoholic addiction as from his orgiastic habits when he does unbend with the bottle. When the Scot goes to get drunk he goes at it wholeheartedly with often the most tiresome and boring results. The appalling drunkenness in the larger Scottish towns before the first war is now happily a thing of the past. It arose and existed almost entirely as a result of the Industrial Revolution and the consequent slum-life. Beer may have been 'the quickest way out of Manchester', but whisky at half-a-crown a bottle was an even quicker way out of the viler parts of Glasgow, Dundee and Edinburgh before the first World War. And the Scot, being who he was, took that quick route as quickly as he could.

This evil is now ended, but the occasional orgiastic habit remains, and it remains in all walks of life. The alcoholic who is addicted to nipping away at the bottle at all hours of the day and night exists in Scotland as elsewhere. On the whole, however, the Scot, even when he has a reputation for hard drinking, confines that hard drinking to set or almost ritual periods.

This comprehensible but on the whole rather uncivilized habit has its effect on, or rather reflects itself in the average public house in Scotland. With a few notable exceptions they are cheerless places where men, and mostly men alone, go for vertical and largely silent drinking. One of the things which pleasantly surprises the young male Scot when he goes South, and particularly to London for the first time, is the friendly, cheerful and respectable nature of the public-houses. There are pleasant pubs in Edinburgh, Glasgow and Aberdeen into which you can without comment or embarrassment take a respectable woman, but they are few and far between. The cosy village pub, nestling beside the ancient village church which is so pleasant a feature of English rural life, is unknown in Scotland.

Conviviality and Hospitality

The above remarks do not mean that there is a lack of conviviality in Scotland. Indeed Scottish conviviality has long been and remains famous. Conviviality and hospitality in Scotland, however, have always tended to go hand in hand. People are convivial in each other's houses rather than in public places. Scottish conviviality can be delightful and civilized, it can also be overpowering. There is a famous story in Dean Ramsay's *Reminiscences of Scottish Life and Character* which is well worth repeating.

Some time in the last century there was a laird's dinner party which began early and ended who knows how many hours later with the continual circulation of the claret bottle. As the pale and haggard light of morning began to press its face against the window, the host noticed that one of his guests was looking ill and had long been silent.

"What gars (makes) the laird of Garscadden look sae gash?" he asked.

"Oh," came the reply from further down the table, "he slippit awa' tae his Makar twa hour syne, but I didnae like tae disturb good company by mentioning it."

Before I go on to talk about conviviality and hospitality today, I cannot forbear quoting from an English traveller's letter from Scotland in the 18th century. The traveller was a curious Captain Burt, and the host whose hospitality he describes in the following was the virtuous and upright Duncan Forbes of Culloden, later Lord President of the Court of Sessions and head of the Scottish legal system:

"There lives in our neighbourhood at a house, or castle called Culloden, a gentleman whose hospitality is almost without bounds. It is the custom of the house, at the first visit or introduction, to take up your freedom by 'cracking his nut', as he terms it, that is a cocoa-shell which holds a pint filled with champagne, or such other sort of wine as you shall choose. Few go away sober at any time; and, for the greatest part of his guests, in the conclusion, they cannot go away at all.

"This he partly brings about by artfully proposing, after the public healths, such private ones as he knows will pique the interest or inclinations of each particular person. . . . As the company are disabled one after another, two servants who are all the while in waiting take up the invalids with short poles in their chairs as they sit (if not fallen down) and carry them to their beds.

"I remember one evening an English officer who has a good deal of humour feigned himself drunk, and acted his part so naturally that it was difficult to distinguish it from reality; upon which the servants were preparing to take him up, and carry him off. He let them alone till they had fixed the machine, and then, raising himself up on his feet, made them a sneering bow, and told them he believed there was no occasion for their assistance. Whereupon one of them with a sangfroid and a serious air said, 'No matter, sir, we shall have you by and by'."

Such scenes, if only on grounds of economy, have long since passed away. They provided in their day, or in the recollections of those who survived them, a fund of good stories. Anyone who is interested in reading about this fantastic trait in the Scottish character in the past is recommended not only to Dean Ramsay's book already mentioned, but to Lord Cockburn's enchanting *Memorials*.

But the tradition of Scottish conviviality and hospitality even in the austerity regime of today goes on. In Edinburgh and Glasgow there are early 19th century and even 18th century dining clubs which continue to flourish. The winter is, of course, the time for these festivities, and the ordinary Scotsman in town, if he has the purse and the taste for it, could spend from October till March in a continuous round of sometimes pawky, sometimes frankly abandoned junketing.

These gatherings are, on the whole, pleasant enough if taken in moderation. Unfortunately, however, they tend to bring out a regrettable trait in the Scottish character—that is after-dinner speaking. The present writer has suffered from American, English and some Continental after-dinner speakers, but he can honestly say that he has never endured from them the half of what he has had to put up with from his compatriots. It is difficult to explain this really painful tendency to post-prandial loquacity amongst a people who in the South of Scotland at least are not much given to words. Maybe the Scot economical with words in private life as he is economical with pence grows prodigal with them in public in the same way in which he can be prodigal with his pounds.

I feel a certain hesitation in referring to Scottish hospitality as it manifests itself in the entertaining of visitors and complete strangers. To praise a quality of this kind in one's compatriots does, even at second-hand, seem slightly to reduce the value of it. Nevertheless, Scottish hospitality to all who come within Scotland's borders is so famous that it is impossible not to mention it.

Having endeavoured to protect myself in this way against the charge of boasting, I venture on the statement that there is no country in Western Europe where a visitor could live freely for a longer time on the hospitality of the people. Maybe with the speed of modern travel and the rush of visitors everywhere to every country every summer this free hospitality in Scotland must decline or at least be more circumspect. But it still exists and flourishes. It is to be found in the towns, but is, of course, most obvious in the country.

Most of this love of giving hospitality springs genuinely from generous hearts. There is, I suspect, also another reason for its origin in the past. Before the days of quick travel Scotland lay very much on the inaccessible fringe of Europe. Quite frankly we were rather flattered when people visited us, and we liked to show our gratitude by the lavishness of our hospitality.

When, shortly after the war, the now famous International Festival of Music and Drama began to be held in Edinburgh, many people smiled at the idea of the grey magnificent but grim old Metropolis of the North acting as hostess to such a venture. They were soon undeceived.

Edinburgh, even the Edinburgh of the austerity years of 1947 and '48 'went to town' in a really astonishing way to greet her visitors. The cab-drivers, the porters, the hotel-servants, the landladies, and above all, the ordinary people in the street from whom the visitors asked the way, may not have had much interest in opera and international drama, but they certainly had a great interest in making their guests feel at home in the Capital of Scotland. You felt that they wanted them to like Edinburgh; and the feeling was infectious. Everyone noticed it.

The Edinburgh Festival has now become an established routine event not only in the Capital of Scotland but in Europe. The first fine careless flush of hospitality on the part of the citizens of Scotland's capital may have died down a bit, the spirit remains.

The Dance

One could go on for a very long time talking about the 'Pleasures and Civilities' as they appear to us in Scotland, even if not all of them appear pleasurable or civil to the foreigner, but one must stop somewhere. A fitting conclusion would seem to be 'the Dance'. It is fitting because it is a form of pleasurable civility which by no means many visitors would associate with Scotland; yet the Dance is one of the most characteristic expressions of the Scottish temperament in certain moods.

By the Dance I do not mean the ordinary modern ballroom dancing which is neither more nor less popular in Scotland than elsewhere. I refer to the perhaps slightly unfortunately named 'Scottish Country Dance' which may have had its origin far back in rural festivities, but is now mostly enjoyed in the towns and big cities.

Let the English reader expel from his mind any idea that the Scottish Country Dance is on the same footing as Morris dancing or folk-lore dancing in the South.

Without wishing to denigrate the admirable movement for the revival of old English traditional dances, one can surely say that it would be impossible to claim for such movements widespread popularity. They are the pleasure of English country lovers of antiquity. Your ordinary English peasant has centuries ago forgotten how to perform in them. And as for the average English town-dweller, he has probably never heard of them.

This is most certainly not true of the traditional Scottish dances. In the cities, in small towns, in village halls and in remote country places there is no more popular form of a dance than the reel with its variations or one of the many other set dances of both Lowland and Highland origin.

By some miracle, the Scottish dance, one of the most lively and national of all the country dances of Europe, managed to survive the long era of Scottish repressive Puritanism. They were dancing reels in the Highlands and in the Lowlands before the Reformation, they danced them somehow, somewhere in the country places and even in some of the towns during the grim 17th century. They most certainly continued to dance them during the 18th century when it might have been supposed that such 'crudities' would have been abandoned in the general attempt at apeing the refined manners of the South—even Boswell, the great lover of London, footed it well at the reel—and they danced them throughout the 19th century down till today; today, when the Scottish Country dance is more popular than ever.

So many other manifestations of the Scottish spirit were driven underground during this era of Puritanism, the theatre, music, and any light form of literature, that it is strange that this one fact of the Scottish dance should have survived, and survived so vigorously. Perhaps it was because the Scottish dance was so purely an indigenous thing, so native an expression of the Scottish spirit that the Puritans were unable to suppress it. They could drive out foreign influences of which they disapproved, but they could not, it appears, utterly suppress a pleasure which the Scot had invented purely for himself.

I am tempted to try to describe the exhilarating experience of dancing in or even only watching an evening of this kind of entertainment. Such pleasures, however, are incommunicable in words. Let me evade the attempt by quoting something I wrote some years ago. It said what I felt then and what I feel now:

> "In its passionate formality, in its blending of abandon and style, in its rhythm of colour and pattern it expresses the Scottish spirit as almost nothing else does. Were I to be asked to *show* Scotland to a foreigner for one evening I would show him the Scottish Dance. But how, alas! can it be shown in writing?"

Yes, I agree with myself. If you want to understand the Scot—the dour inhibited Scot, the expressive romantic Scot, the happy Scot, the melancholy Scot, the Scot of any kind whatsoever, you cannot do so completely until you have seen him (and her) dancing the traditional native dances of the country.

Chapter Four

Language and Other Differences

Accent

"WHAT a strong English accent he's picked up!" These words, though spoken when I was a small boy and just before the first World War, are as clear in the ear of my memory as if they had been uttered yesterday. They were spoken by a Spartan and spinster aunt of mine about me and in my hearing to my mother after my family had been abroad and in the South for a year or two. I was only about ten or eleven at the time, but I had come back from travel to our comfortable mildly prosperous professional family existence in Scotland, bearing with me an 'English accent'. I can honestly say that I felt a trifle ashamed of myself—as if I had been guilty of some social *gaffe*.

It is extremely unlikely that today even the most Spartan Scottish spinster aunt in a family of prosperous well-educated circumstances would utter such a remark about a small nephew or that the small nephew should feel abashed by it. Thirty years of the radio, five years of television, quick travel and the general disturbances of life caused by two world wars have since 1914 so mixed up the speech in these islands that no Scottish small boy of the educated classes could seriously be ashamed of having acquired an 'English accent'.

Nevertheless it was once not so, and not so very long ago either. After all, 1914 was well into the second decade of this century. At that time there was a number of highly educated Scots folk, especially elderly ladies, who had travelled much and heard much who regarded *their* use of the language which they shared with the English as the correct or at least more pleasing one. They regarded the Scottish intonation and pronunciation of words, particularly those containing h and r, as being more careful, decent and more ladylike, or more gentlemanly, than what seemed to them the slovenly and affected Southern English use. Some of this tradition of pride in the Scottish use of speech still lingers occasionally in educated and upper-class circles in Scotland, but it is (and I cannot help feeling sorry for it) on the way out.

A proper pride amongst the educated classes in the Scottish accent as being at least the equal of the English accent may, under the pressure of radio and TV, be on the way out, but the matter of language remains none-the-less one of the most obvious differences between the English and the Scots. It remains, incidentally, a matter of considerable internal difference within Scotland itself. To understand the Scot at home you must, even if you can't always understand what he is saying, understand *about* his language.

The Three Scottish Tongues

There are three different spoken languages in Scotland today. The most ancient is, of course, Gaelic. The most modern is English—whether it be spoken in an English or Scottish style and manner. In between in point of time there is the old Scots tongue which survives in Lowland country districts and lies not so very far under the surface of much working-class speech in the towns.

The Gaelic

Since no one who picks up this little book is likely to put himself to the trouble of learning Gaelic—one of the most difficult tongues in Western Europe to acquire—there is not much point in saying more about it than this. It is one of the oldest of living languages. It is highly expressive, poetic, full of imaginative nuances, yet has been also much used as a martial masculine means of expression. If, however, you overhear people in the Western Highlands or islands talking Gaelic amongst themselves it may at first sound to you guttural rather than liquid. Its true quality is shown nevertheless in the effect on those who speak it when they turn to English.

The English of a native-born Gaelic speaker is one of the pleasantest forms of speaking that language that exists. It is soft, delicate, poetic in sound, yet often humorous in effect. It is as far removed from what is known as a 'Scotch accent' as is the English of an Irish peasant which it slightly resembles. It is, however, softer than Irish English, and for anyone who has an ear for the differences of speech, there could be no confusion between the two. As mentioned in an earlier chapter, it is spoken in the West and in the islands. It is fighting a gallant battle against modern conditions, but is alas! indubitably losing ground. It will be a sad day for Scotland if it ever dies out. Indeed Scotland will scarcely be Scotland then.

The 'Guid Scots Tongue'

With regard to the other native Scottish language, the old Scots tongue, I beg the reader not to think I am being merely pedantic when I claim for it the right of a separate language. It would be possible (though, in a light-hearted essay of this nature, highly inappropriate) to make out a scholarly case for the differing though parallel growths of the English and Scots language—or rather the growth of one and decline of the other; but that would be tedious. No, what I mean by saying that the Scots tongue is a separate language is that certain people in certain districts of Scotland will *consciously* talk Scots amongst themselves, using many words that would be incomprehensible to an Englishman. The same people can switch over into straight English, with a Scottish accent, of course, when talking to a Southerner.

If anyone whose normal speech is English doubts the essential difference between his speech and Scots, let him listen to a group of Aberdeenshire farmers on market-day in some town in the North-East. He will not understand one quarter of what is being said. I have heard English people in such circumstances say that they could not understand anything. But there is a simpler test. Most English people know some lines from the more famous lyrics of Burns, such as 'My luve is like a red, red rose', and certainly these are not incomprehensible. But if they care to look at some of the longer and less well-known poems, I will guarantee that they will be much baffled. Burns after all died only four years before the beginning of the 19th century, and he was not consciously writing in an antique style but in the living language of his own Ayrshire.

Is this language really surviving or has it just sunk into the position of a peasant *patois* due for departure? The answer is that it most certainly does survive and has, as I shall shortly hope to show, odd injections of vitality put into it from time to time from the most unexpected quarters. But it has, of course, socially declined in status and like the Gaelic, but for different reasons, is probably on the way out.

The main reason for its decline from a general spoken language into a private language is due to social causes. Children at home will talk Scots, but at school they are taught English. If they want to get on in the world they know that they must rely on English and tend to thrust their family and native tongue into the background. But it *does* remain in the background. In such places as Aberdeenshire the background is not very far back. Further South and in the big cities it is, of course, much overlaid. Nevertheless it is still there. I would like to illustrate this by two examples.

A few years after the war, the Citizens' Theatre founded in Glasgow by the late and much-lamented James Bridie put on Mr. Robert McLellan's admirable play *Jamie the Saxt* about the Scottish King James VI before he succeeded to the English throne as James I. It was written (except for the small part of the English Ambassador) entirely in Scots, and some of it in rather old-fashioned, if not exactly period Scots at that. There were gloomy prophecies before the first night. Who, it was asked, in a great modern industrial city such as Glasgow, would understand such a play, save possibly a few scholars or cranks? I myself attended a dress rehearsal and had my doubts too. There were words here and there that bamboozled me. What would the public think?

The public of the great modern industrial city of Glasgow gave their answer: they lapped it up for three weeks and could have taken much more had not other plays been scheduled. Now I do not say that everyone who filled the theatre understood all the words in this play, but they did understand most of them and, from some deep consciousness in them, *felt* those that they did not immediately comprehend. It is in no spirit of condescension that one says that it is doubtful if an intelligent London critic could have followed more than half of the play. The people of Glasgow followed it because something out of the background of their own childhood responded to it. It was, I repeat, also a most excellent drama.

The other example I would like to quote is something that happened in the most matter-of-fact little town of Kirriemuir in the East Lowlands. That amiable and highly scholarly eccentric Mr. Douglas Young, Classics Lecturer at St. Andrews University, was in some small public hall where a number of business men and farmers had gathered, and he was being cross-questioned by them. The subject of his cross-questioning was the fact that he wrote his poetry deliberately in the Old Scots Tongue. Was not this, so it was put to him, an affectation for a polyglot scholar whose normal speech was English?

For an answer Douglas, black-bearded, thin, attenuated, rather odd-looking (just the sort of figure the average dour Lowlander might have dismissed as a *poseur*) rose to his full six and a half feet and recited a few lines. The lines he spoke were those of the 23rd Psalm, 'The Lord is my shepherd', but he spoke them in his Scots version, or translation as you will, which he himself had made.

Now there is no Psalm, indeed it would be difficult to think of any other piece of prose, more familiar to the Scottish ear and heart than 'The Lord is my shepherd'. All these Lowland farmers and country-town business men had heard and repeated the 23rd Psalm since their earliest childhood, but they had heard and repeated it in Church or Sunday School *in English.* Now, for the first time, they heard this most familiar Psalm repeated in what was to them really familiar language, the language of their families in childhood. The effect, so an onlooker told me, was immediate. These hard, matter-of-fact Scotsmen from the Lowland town of Kirriemuir were touched to the heart and showed it. There were tears in some eyes.

The mention of this serious drama *Jamie the Saxt*, written in Scots, and the poetic scholarly Scots version of the 23rd Psalm leads to an interesting recent development in the Scots tongue. I mentioned earlier that the language usually regarded now as a peasant *patois* has had of late odd injections of vitality. This has come from the unexpected source of the scholars and the poets.

There has been some admirable scholarly work done in research into the language and with the idea of helping to preserve it. By far the most significant poetry that has been composed in Scotland for the last thirty years has been in the Scots tongue. The claims of certain native born Scottish poets to be able to express themselves not only more fluently but with deeper feeling in Scots than in English certainly seem to be justified by results. All this it is claimed is a part of the Nationalist movement in art and literature which began to manifest itself after the first World War. But of this I should like to speak in my last chapter.

Finally, though there has been some attempt on the part of the scholars to give a form and standard to the language in so far as it still exists, they are up against a larger problem than they can tackle. Your Lowland Scot is an intense individualist, and in nothing more so than in his language. For four centuries the Old Scots tongue has lived on, but, if not exactly underground, only in private and family circumstances. This means that there is an immense variation in the way that it is spoken. I have said that an Englishman would not understand scarcely anything of what he heard at a gathering of Aberdeenshire farmers. I am bound to admit that a Border farmer, or one from Galloway in the extreme South-West of the country might find some difficulty himself in a remote Aberdeenshire village.

Scots English

The 'Scotch accent' as portrayed in England is almost purely a music-hall invention of the comedians. "Hoots mon" . . . The wee hoose 'mang the heatherrr . . . and so on to an infinite rolling of rs is supposed to be the way the ordinary Scot talks English. An extremely painful and embarrassing experience is to hear an amiable Englishman when in Scotland trying to put on such an accent, partly for fun maybe, and partly to make the natives feel at ease. As an embarrassing sound it is only equalled, I must admit, by the attempts of many a Scot to speak what he thinks is 'high English'.

Still, there is a Scots form of English which it would be correct to describe as English with a Scots accent, intonation and style. In the days of my boyhood it was spoken by nearly all of the educated, prosperous or well-to-do professional classes as well as by some of what we have now been taught to call 'U speakers' or members of the indubitable upper classes. Today, of course, it still very much exists. But the habit which even comparatively well-to-do people have acquired of sending their sons to English public schools at their most formative years has tended to reduce it.

It was and is a pleasant form of English. The rs are pronounced but not, of course, rolled in the music-hall manner, nor are they ever 'intrusive' as in 'Indiar-office'. The hs after the letter w, as in why, when, what and where, are always sounded. (All Scotsmen sound these hs even to this day. The dropping of them sounds to us, not so much English as positively Cockney.) It is on the whole a precise, formal and meticulous form of speech, sometimes so meticulous as to smack of pedantry. It can, when not sounding pedantic, be homely and expressive. Many a learned Scottish advocate at the bar, or a Scottish Judge of the old-fashioned school of speech, has owed his success in dealing with witnesses to his Scottish manner of voice. The humble and often terrified occupant of the witness stand would be put off by the condescension of an advocate or Judge talking to him in real 'broad Scots', but when he is addressed in Scots-English he does not feel he is necessarily being talked to from another world of privilege, power and money. In other words, he is being talked to by one of his own countrymen.

Alas! this decent old-fashioned Scots-English can become supremely ridiculous when the speaker is trying to turn it into high English. The vowel a is a perpetual trap for such aspirants. Originally all Scottish a's were long; there was no such thing as a short a spoken by a Scotsman even in such words as hat and man. The

Scottish speaker endeavouring to converse in high English is aware of the fact that in England the a is sometimes long and sometimes short, but he is never quite sure when it is short and when long. He sometimes says 'Sāturday ăfternoon' or 'gās-măsk'. I have never been fortunate enough to hear the two phrases used together, though I have often steered the conversation to that end, but without result.

All apeing of refinement in speech is ridiculous wherever practised and in whatever language. It is, however, particularly ridiculous in a native-born speaker of English in the Scottish manner. The true Scottish accent or style of speech is virile, homely, forthright and precise. When someone attempts to refine upon it the fall into absurdity is even greater than in other forms of English. Moreover the subjects mentioned in Scottish speech are often so homely and ordinary that to refine upon them is to make the refinement sound all the more grotesque, thus:
upon it the fall into absurdity even greater than in other forms of English refinement. Moreover the subjects mentioned in Scottish speech are often so homely and ordinary that to refine upon them is to make the refinement sound all the more grotesque, thus:

When I was a young man in the 1920s I visited the then newly-founded 'Palais de Danse' in Edinburgh. Having selected my partner from the 'pen' of professional dancers I trundled her round the room in some youthful embarrassment, not knowing quite what to say. Eventually the poor lassie broke the silence and ice by saying: "Do you perspaire? Ai do freely."

Other Differences—The Law

It is not generally known outside Scotland (except

for the marriage customs and the Gretna Green runaways) that an entirely separate and different legal system from that in the rest of the British Isles operates in Scotland. The Scot is very proud of his law which derives from Roman sources, instead of, as in England, from Anglo-Norman ecclesiastical origins. Sometimes this pride is justified, sometimes not.

Still, to understand the Scot you must know something about the differences between English and Scottish law, if only to be forewarned should you get into trouble North of the Border. I am no lawyer, and I give here only those differences which are most obvious and which have cropped up before me in my writing and journalistic life. For what they are worth I give an ordinary man's comments on these differences.

Suicide is no crime in Scotland. You cannot be charged with attempted suicide. *But* if you do have a shot at killing yourself and are unsuccessful you are nearly always pulled in, perhaps not publicly, for committing a public nuisance or endangering the peace. One Sheriff (roughly the Scottish equivalent of a Recorder or paid magistrate in England) said in my hearing to a young friend of mine who had been so foolish as to attempt suicide, but who had recovered, the following unforgettable words:

"Young man, in this country of Scotland you can commit suicide as often as you please, but you mustn't make a nuisance of yourself. In this instance you have made a great nuisance of yourself to your friends and to a number of His Majesty's officials whose duty it is to keep the peace."

This was just the sort of half joking yet severe homily the youth needed. The Sheriff, with characteristic dry

Scottish humour, ended: "I fine you ten pounds. And don't commit suicide again."

You can make up your own mind on the theoretical, or rather theological, point as to whether a man has the right to take his own life and whether he should be punished for attempting to do so. Scottish law on this point seems, rather uncharacteristically, to evade the issue. It says suicide is not a crime, but those who administer the law always contrive to make an attempt at it a misdemeanour. The English attitude is, for once, more logical.

One most important and beneficial result, however, springs from this attitude towards suicide in Scottish law. Attempted suicides are not tried in public and the misery of the people who have been reduced to such attempts is not increased by public enquiry into why they attempted it.

There is also no Coroner's Inquest in Scotland, with the beneficial result that a suicide's relatives are not distressed by the public revelation of the circumstances which drove him to self-destruction. It is the Procurator Fiscal who enquires into a death by accident. If, with the aid of his staff and the police, he decides that it is a case in which murder or manslaughter might have been committed he makes a report to that effect, in which case a trial takes place. If it is suicide he also makes a report to that effect, but it is not publicized.

So, if you live in the British Isles, and feel you must commit suicide, it would be better to do this wicked and foolish act in Scotland rather than in England. I have sometimes thought of writing a short story in which a conscientious and law-abiding man intent on suicide but living in England takes the train across the Border by Berwick and throws himself out of the express immediately after Berwick. Unfortunately he forgets that the Scottish-English Border runs three miles North of Berwick. So, posthumously, he breaks the law and has to submit to a Coroner's Inquest after all.

One very important point of difference in Scottish and English law concerns the public pre-knowledge of the trial of those accused of serious crimes. In England a murderer's case is heard *in public* before a magistrate before it goes to the Old Bailey. The public, therefore, in a sensational case know from the press all the fruity details before the case comes for real trial. In Scotland a murderer is not tried twice in public. It is, therefore, more easy to pick a truly unbiassed Jury.

I daresay the merits or demerits of these various differences could be argued by those more expert than I am. I do venture to assert, however, that in two points the Scottish legal system is perhaps inferior. We have three verdicts: Guilty, Not Guilty and Not Proven. What is the sense of Not Proven? Is it not just an easy way out for Juries who can't make up their minds? The practical result is just the same as Not Guilty. Someone once said, however, that its meaning was "Not Guilty, but don't do it again." Before the Union there were only two verdicts in Scottish law—Guilty or Not Proven. It was the unfortunate imitation or the introduction of the Southern verdict as well, i.e. Not Guilty, which made this confusion and was responsible for what seems to most of us an inferiority in Scottish law.

Greatly daring I also venture to criticize the Scottish system of majority verdicts by Jury. Our Juries are composed of fifteen members and a verdict can be arrived at by a bare majority of one, i.e. seven against six. It is, I suggest, risky in important cases such as murder for the result to rest on one vote; it is surely better for twelve persons to be unanimous, or, if they can't agree, to have the trial again. It is true that if, in a murder case the prisoner (or panel in Scotland) is found guilty on a majority verdict of one his sentence is reconsidered by the Secretary of State and is usually reduced. But the fact of the verdict being arrived at by so small a majority is not made public, and the subsequent reconsideration and reduction is all carried out in a rather hole-and-corner manner.

On the whole, however, the Roman-derived Scottish legal system is slightly more inclined in the accused's favour than is the English. So, if you are thinking of getting yourself accused of something, not only attempted suicide, cross the Border to the North, and be accused in our hospitable land.

Humour

The difference between the English and Scottish sense of what is funny is large, so large that there is a notion in England that the Scots have no sense of humour at all. The enchanting and lovable Sydney Smith put the Englishman's point of view about this into one famous saying, "It takes a surgical operation to get a joke into a Scotsman's head."

How well one knows what he meant! The typical Lowland Scot *can* display a most depressing habit of taking one's most trivial and lightest flights of verbal fancy literally. Everyone who has been in Scotland, everyone who has met a certain type of Scot abroad must have had experience of this tendency. Sometimes it is sheer boneheadedness, an inability to perceive the English form of humour. Sometimes, however, it is not boneheadedness but a deliberate and dry attempt to show disapproval. In neither case, however, should the fact that the Scot can't or won't appreciate English humour be taken to mean that he hasn't got a form of humour of his own.

The Scot (and I really must repeat that in this context I am speaking about the Lowland Scot) loves his humour to be laconic and sometimes macabre. He thinks death is funny, and the stories about the humour of death in Scotland are numberless. The one which I have already recounted about the Laird of Garscadden dying during a prolonged dinner-party is typical. Undertakers are stock figures of fun on the Scottish music-hall stage and in popular plays. Perhaps it is because I am Highland rather than Lowland in blood and have spent much of my life travelling and away from Scotland, but I cannot say that I relish these music-hall turns or popular-play characters, though some of the Scottish death or corpse stories are sufficiently far-removed from reality to be funny.

It is difficult to know why the Lowland Scot finds death and the solemn appurtenances of death to be funny. He is a kindly, family-loving and, as has been amply demonstrated, sentimental fellow at heart. He would never cruelly expose anyone who had suffered a bereavement to mockery, but in the abstract he does find mortality amusing. The most charitable view that one can take is that the Scot is so fundamentally religious-minded, even when he is not kirk-going, that he believes unshakeably in the immortality of the soul, and finds the fuss made over departure from the flesh and the earth humorous. Maybe there are other and less flattering reasons to account for this streak in Scottish humour, but I can't think of them.

Apart from jokes about death or disaster, the Scot likes his humour to be dry, self-contained, unornamented, and often depending on one single word. He likes to tell his tales with a dead-pan face, and does not expect or even like them to be received with noisy acclamation. He prefers to savour his own humour slowly, rolling it round the palate of his mind before swallowing it, and without ostentation. Of the laconic tales depending on one word, my favourite is this one.

A shy young minister of the kirk was introducing the various items at a village concert in the North-East of Scotland. When the concert was about halfway through he consulted his notes and, still nervously, announced:

"And noo, ladies and gentlemen, Miss Jeannie Macpherson will sing 'The Flo'ers o' the Forest'."

He was interrupted by an alcoholic voice shouting from the back of the hall, "Jeannie Macpherson's a whüre." (harlot).

The poor little minister fumbled with his notes even more nervously and then, clearing his throat, said:

"Nevertheless, Miss Jeannie Macpherson will noo sing 'The Flo'ers o' the Forest'."

In telling this characteristic Scottish story which can 'nevertheless' be attempted by any Saxon raconteur, it is important to remember to roll the 'r' in the one operative word.

Minor Differences of Use and Custom

The Scottish male is meticulous in addressing all other males, until he becomes friendly or intimate with them, by their designation. He does not, from whatever class he comes, like addressing a peer or a Judge, apart obviously from Court occasions, as 'My Lord'. He will carefully call him Lord So and So, but not 'My Lord'. He will equally carefully give the Mr. to all his associates, however long he may have known them, until he feels intimate enough to use their Christian names. He particularly dislikes the English habit of calling a man Smith or Macdonald or whatever his surname may be without some form of designation or prefix. The use of the surname alone in Scotland and spoken by a Scottish voice sounds to him to be either insolent (and particularly insolent if addressed to someone lower in the social scale than the speaker) or as if the speaker were imitating English Public School manners.

Scottish public houses are officially closed on Sundays. A merciful pre-1914 regulation, now moribund in England, still fortunately survives for the benefit of what is called bona-fide travellers; that is, those who have moved in a journey on Sunday over a distance of more than three miles. In theory then any public house which has a 'seven-day licence' or any licensed hotel is supposed to serve anyone who can prove that he is travelling from one minute past midnight on Saturday until one minute to midnight on Sunday.*

Obviously this charitable dispensation cannot be universally enforced. Seven-day licence pubs on Sundays now tend to keep normal week-day opening hours, even though they are not compelled by law to do so. They do, however, have to present the bona-fide drinker with a book in which he enters his name, address, the place he came from and his destination. Provided such formalities are not grossly abused, the police turn a blind eye to the fact that many a thirsty man will walk, bicycle or drive three miles on the Sabbath for no other reason than that of getting a drink.

*Please see page 79

The ‘bona fide’ traveller can get a drink all
the 24 hours of Sunday

Before the last war some hotel-keepers generously and strictly tried to serve all travellers at all times on Sundays. I remember a red-headed Highlander on the road North who regretfully turned us out of his hotel bar at ten o'clock on Saturday night with the consoling words, "Come back at midnight, lads. The Sabbath begins then and you can drink for twenty-four hours till you're ready to go on with your journey." But that was in 1937. Those, alas! are days of the past.

I have seen, and have myself made, some strange entries into the bona-fide travellers' book which must be signed before a drink is served. "From Athens, Greece, to Athens, Wisconsin," is one place of origin and destination which I have successfully filled in. Once I saw in the entry above me the note of a traveller "From the cradle to the grave." The absurdity of this law used in pre-war days and as late as until 1939 to be made manifest by the numbers of thirsty Englishmen who in certain places would cross the Border on the Sabbath to drink out of English hours in Scotland.

I have included this oddity of Sunday drinking under the heading of minor differences. I am not sure, however, that, in its indication of some important elements in the Scottish character, that it deserves the epithet minor. Scottish puritanism is a strong trait in our character, and even in these days can make its influence powerfully felt. At war with this puritanism is the average Scot's individual hatred of being ordered about to suit other people's inclinations or beliefs. But there is another and significant Scottish trait which keeps the now admittedly obsolescent bona-fide laws still operative. That is his love of sticking to his 'rights'.

Some time in the 19th century the Puritan element in Scotland succeeded not only in closing all public houses in the country on Sundays, but even preventing the sale of liquor in hotels. In the days of horse travel (for the regulation came into force before the railway) some concession simply had to be made for travellers on the long and often bare and exposed Scottish roads; and so the 'bona-fide' exception clause was introduced. But, the concession having been granted, a sacred 'right of man' was introduced. The Scot pertinaciously and pedantically sticks to his 'rights'. A more easy-going people might have allowed the 'bona-fide' right to slip away from them in the general invasion of personal privileges which followed the end of the first war. Not so the Scot. Even though the bona-fide fiction has become an absurdity, it remains a 'right'.

Otherwise the ridiculous licensing laws that a 'British Parliament' forced on the unfortunate English after 1918 are the same in Scotland as in the Southern Kingdom. I do not think it is because I am particularly thirsty or particularly Chauvinistic, but it does seem to me that there is more generally tolerated evasion of these licensing laws in Scotland. By this I do not mean back-door drinking or surreptitious nips in the hotel parlour when no one is looking. Any respectable inhabitant of the larger Scottish cities knows in these cities a number of equally respectable hotels where he can get a drink at any reasonable time for the asking—and get it served too in the public rooms.

The police apparently know that this 'privilege of evasion' is not being abused by the hotel-keeper for the sake of drunkards, and presumably wink at it. One must in fairness point out that the casual visitor to Scotland or to any particular Scottish town cannot expect the privilege of evasion. One has to be known by name to be served in this manner.

But how preposterous it all is! I speak here not as a Scot but as an inhabitant of Great Britain, subject to Westminster-made laws. How long are we going to put up with such pettifogging regulations as the licensing laws which are no more than a long survival from the Defence of the Realm Act of the first World War?

One could continue in detail, giving a list of many other small 'differences' which the traveller from the South may notice in Scotland. Married women are called Mistress instead of Mrs. (Mistress Macdonald, not Mrs. Macdonald). Country communities are scattered rather than gathered together in villages in the pleasant English habit. Country architecture is of stone, and one misses the warm glow of 18th century English brick. In the towns, however, this stone building can produce, as it obviously does in Edinburgh, a grand and massive effect. The country public houses are, as has already been mentioned, generally graceless and cheerless. The 19th century architecture of most country churches is a disgrace and contrasts painfully with the rich glories of the English village church. But there are other differences which small though they may be will please the visitor—the freedom of the countryside, the general lack of 'fencing-in', the freedom of sporting facilities and so on. But it is more proper that the visitor should find out these minor differences for himself than that they should be mentioned here. This chapter must have an end some time.

Publisher's note: Readers will, no doubt, be vastly relieved to learn that since the first appearance of this book the licensing authorities have seen fit to liberalise the law relating to the sale of drink on Sundays. Although public houses still remain closed on the Sabbath, hotels may serve alcohol without the necessity of patrons registering as bona-fide travellers.

Chapter Five

The Scot Abroad and at Home

Abroad

THE usual phrase 'at home and abroad' is here reversed for the simple reason that there are said to be far more Scots outside their own country than in it.

My amiable and scholarly friend, Douglas Young of St. Andrews University, already referred to, puts the number of Scots abroad as high as twenty-two million. Douglas is not only amiable and scholarly but exact, and not given to rash statements. I have never pressed him for a definition of a Scot abroad. Does he mean people of Scottish blood living out of Scotland yet separated by two or more generations? Does he confine his definition to those bearing Scottish names? Would he include the fourth generation Gaelic-speaking inhabitants of Nova Scotia originally descended from the emigrants who were driven from their homes nearly 200 years ago? Would his net capture the scattered descendants of the more fortunately placed (at least less persecuted) Scots who settled in Carolina, but who are now to all appearances American gentlemen from the South?

I don't know for sure; but he has arrived at some definition that satisfies him. Let us be more exigent and just halve his estimated number without further enquiry. That still leaves eleven million Scots abroad and only five million at home!

This is an extraordinary state of affairs which you can interpret either to the credit or the discredit of the Scottish character as you please. It is indeed lamentable that Scotland, full of vast open spaces of land from which the emigrants were once driven, land which is still capable of development either agriculturally or industrially, should have sent so disproportionate a number of her sons abroad. On the other hand the Scottish love of adventure and enterprise which discovers itself in this wandering spirit is no bad thing; and the Scot certainly does wander.

The Wandering Scot

A Scottish shipwrecked sailor, so it is said, found himself washed up on some remote South Sea isle in the last century. He was captured, held under control, but fairly kindly treated by the natives. Eventually he was taken into their temple to witness a religious ceremony. The High Priest, or half-god, who presided over the ceremonies passed through the kneeling crowds, scattering his benedictions, mumbling some incantation the while. As he passed him the sailor was startled to hear in the homely accents of his own native town of Scotland the following words repeated over and over again: "If it does ye nae guid it'll dae ye nae harm . . . if it does ye nae guid it'll dae ye nae harm."

It turned out that the half-god was no other than his old friend Sam Mackay who had been wandering the face of the earth for years and had eventually found some kind of a home on this remote island. He allowed himself to be worshipped by "thae puir ignorant savages" but placated his Presbyterian conscience by the form of his incantation "If it does ye nae guid it'll dae ye nae harm."

This apochryphal tale is typical of many stories, some true, some just fantastic, which illustrate the Scot's capacity for turning up in odd places in any corner of the world. Any Scot who has himself been about a bit, as the saying goes, must have had experiences of meeting his countrymen or the descendants of his countrymen in the most unexpected circumstances. In Poland (when I was allowed to go there before the war and was not on any 'forbidden list') I came across a number of Scots who were the descendants of mercenary soldiers during the 17th and 18th centuries. Though most of them could only speak Polish they consciously kept the fact of their Scottish descent ever present in their minds. Their names, though now spelt and pronounced in the Slavonic manner, obviously retained their Scottish origins.

I have come across the descendants of the old wandering Scots who kept their names and sometimes their religion as well as something of their language in nearly every country in Europe which I have visited. Admittedly I have a curiosity about such national types and often took some trouble in nosing them out. Still, they were there to find. I have, of course, also come across innumerable native-born Scots who have settled down all over Europe. They have been good at acquiring languages, but are obstinately conservative about not 'going native': they cling characteristically and Scottishly to their native traditions.

The European wandering Scot, whether of first generation or far removed in time from the land of his origin, is the inheritor of an admirable tradition. It is the tradition that sent the poor scholars in the Middle Ages from the impoverished little country in the North to seek learning in the great universities of Europe. It is the tradition that sent out explorers, missionaries, soldiers of repute and soldiers of fortune to all parts of the earth.

Such men left Scotland in the past centuries sometimes because their native land was too poor to offer them the opportunities their ardent spirits craved for; nevertheless they kept their Scottishness about them as closely and as obviously as did any wandering Jew. In those days they never attempted to denationalize themselves. Such wandering Scots have often appeared in descriptive memoirs and in fiction. One of the best characters of this type in a novel is Lieutenant Lismahago in Smollett's 'Humphrey Clinker'.

These men left Scotland in the past, it should also be remembered, not only for gain or for larger opportunities. Often, as did David Livingstone, they took themselves and the better qualities of their nationality into the larger world out of a genuine love for humanity. Still, the inescapable fact remains that they left their mother country (who had given them so much), the poorer for their absence. Having set that sentence down it smacks to me ever so slightly of cant. However, having seen so much of the best of Scotland drained away from Scotland even during my own lifetime, I do not feel inclined to withdraw it. I do admit nonetheless that to try and make the Scot a stay-at-home and to cure him of his wandering habits would be to attempt the impossible.

Heid o' the Depairtment

"Wherever you go in England or the Commonwealth

you'll find a Scot head of a department in every organisation." How often has one not heard this complacent boast uttered by Scottish business men! But when you examine it what does it mean, save that the pertinacious, assiduous Scot of an administrative turn of mind has the capacity for becoming second in command in the English speaking world, but seldom first. 'The heid o' the depairtment' (thus spelt because the Scottishness in speech of these gentlemen is often a highly saleable quality) outside Scotland is often an admirable fellow. He is honest, hard-working, a disciplinarian without being too severe and is, above everything else, reliable. Those in charge of large affairs know that they can leave the detailed running of departmental matters safely in his hands.

As such he is presumably a good advertisement for the country which he has left to better himself. It cannot be said, however, that as a type he is particularly attractive. If the wandering European Scots, or those who turn up in odd and remote corners of the world, are descendants of the romantic travelling Scots of past centuries, the heid o' the depairtment has another and less appealing ancestry. His forerunners were the needy Scots who after the Union cleared out of their own country to seek wealth in the richer lands of the South or in the then expanding British Empire.

These needy Scots who in the 18th and early 19th centuries descended upon the South or went overseas to become heads of Imperial departments were not usually popular in the lands of their adoption. In the 18th century indeed in London they were extremely unpopular—rather undeservedly so, for they were only the products of a political movement over which they had had no control. One does not, therefore, wish to say anything unfair about them, but it is possible, even at this distance, to see why they were not liked.

They were clannish, reserved, apparently ungenerous and suspicious. These failings sprang from a psychological need to defend themselves from a slight sense of guilt. They wanted to keep the advantages of their Scottish birth and the advantages of possessing the Scottish character, but at the same time they could not conceal from themselves that they had left their own native country, in which they constantly expressed such pride, under their own impulse and solely for gain.

Sometimes they clung ostentatiously to their Scottish characteristics of speech, manner and custom, sometimes they tried to get rid of these as well as they could. Those who went to London succeeded after a fashion in one or two generations in becoming English. Others who went overseas pushed their background even further from them. Such second generation Scots in Canada, for instance, often give considerable lip-service to their Scottish ancestry but are haters of the European tradition which made the Scotland on which they or their fathers turned their backs. A dynamic example of a Scottish-Canadian-European-culture-hater is, of course, Lord Beaverbrook, but then he is a heid o' a depairtment of genius. He has made his own department of which he is head and has straddled the world with it. In his virtues and his failings he is 'the type' pushed to the Nth degree. And how he dislikes Europe!

The heid o' a depairtment abroad in the English-speaking world tends to exaggerate in himself the national qualities which his countrymen are supposed to possess. He is usually particularly dour and non-committal. He flaunts his Old Testament philosophy, but can on suitable occasions (Burns's nights, for instance) display that capacity for sentiment with which the Lowlander can so often surprise the foreigner. I cannot say that the heid o' a depairtment abroad is a type that appeals to me. If I have been unfair to him I apologize. He has many sterling qualities.

We in Dreams behold the Hebrides

There was a short poem published anonymously in an Edinburgh magazine a hundred and thirty years ago about the emigrant Scots of Highland descent in Canada. One quatrain of it has become famous. I make no apology for quoting it here once again, for it cannot be too often written down, re-read and recalled; it has the peculiar magic which occasional verse sometimes possesses:

"*From the lone shieling of the misty island*
Mountains divide us and a waste of seas;
But still the blood is strong, the heart is Highland,
And we in dreams behold the Hebrides."

Never in the English language has the longing of the genuinely exiled Scot for his homeland been more poignantly expressed. When I say 'genuinely exiled' I mean those who were turned out of their country by persecution or the force of circumstances, either political or economic, rather than those who left Scotland merely to benefit themselves.

These genuinely exiled Scots were nearly all Highlanders who were turned out of their land at the time of the Clearances beginning in the 18th century and continuing to a period well within living memory at the end of the 19th. The vast majority of these who had to endure this enforced exile went across the Atlantic to Canada, or the United States. Their devotion to the land which they had been compelled to leave was genuine, sincere and deeply felt.

They realized that in most cases their parting from Scotland was, for them and their children, forever. Nevertheless they took something of their native Highlands with them. Sometimes ministers from dispossessed parishes would accompany their flocks over the Atlantic. And from the Catholic Highlands (where the enforced emigration was particularly severe) priests often went with their people. They also took with them the Gaelic language with the result, as has already been mentioned, that there are more native Gaelic speakers in Nova Scotia today than in all Scotland. These 'Scots abroad' have remained consciously Scots to the third and fourth generations. They acquire, of course, the habits, speech and manners of the country in which they find themselves, but in dreams they still genuinely do 'behold the Hebrides'.

A few years ago a North American priest (not from Nova Scotia, but from somewhere in the U.S.A.) called upon me in Edinburgh with a note of introduction from a friend, asking me to show him the city and, if possible, motor him into the Highlands. This I gladly agreed to do. My visitor bore a Scottish name and explained to me that his great-grandfather had 'originally come from' a certain district in the North-West. He was, however, a typical American ecclesiastic of the more agreeable kind. He was genial, had a fund of good stories, obviously did not lack for money, and, of course, spoke American, but with as pronounced a twang as ever I have heard. I could just imagine the kind of parish over which he presided in New York, or was it Chicago?

As we motored North-West he entertained me vastly

with his cheery ebullience. As we approached the district which was our object, and from where his great-grandfather had been expelled by the then laird, he grew more silent. When we got to the place itself he asked me to stop the car. I did so and the priest got out and, crossing a small croft, began to speak to an old man working on it. When I came up with them I heard to my astonishment that the conversation was being conducted in Gaelic.

Back again in the car I asked him how he had acquired the language. "From my mother and father," he replied. I felt more than a trifle humiliated. My own Highland originating family which had never been uprooted from Scotland had long ago lost the Gaelic. My own few stumbling attempts in the language of my forefathers had been achieved by the deliberate effort of learning—and that not much. Here was the son of an exiled Scottish family who through four generations had kept their native tongue intact, and in the great cities of North America across the Atlantic.

Sometimes this preservation of the Gaelic by exiled emigrants overseas can lead to extraordinary results. South Carolina was a place to which a number of the Highland gentry rather than the Highland crofters went after the political upheavals halfway through the 18th century. They acquired slaves there and taught them Gaelic. It is unlikely that there are any Gaelic-speaking negroes left in the Southern States now. I have heard on good authority, however, that as late as the 1890s there was a church in Caroline attended solely by coloured people and ministered to by a coloured pastor. The language used at the services by these 'all black' worshippers was Gaelic!

It would be too much to claim that these good

Celtic-tongued negroes were exiled Scots, but the fact that they existed at all is a remarkable tribute to the pertinacity with which some genuinely exiled Scots of Highland origin clung to their language not only across the seas but over the centuries. Truly the Scot abroad can be a remarkable individual.

The Scot at Home

This, of course, is a subject which could be treated in a score of different ways. Indeed most of the rest of this essay on 'Understanding the Scots' is about the Scot at home. In this chapter I would like only to deal with the home-staying Scot's attitude towards his native country —not politically or administratively, but emotionally.

The *average* Scot who lives in Scotland has something more than an affection, rather a deep love, and sometimes a passion for the physical fact of Scotland. This emotion, as I believe and as I hope to show, springs from two causes; one out of the distant past, one contemporary.

The inhabitants of every country have a natural love for their own land in the physical sense of the word, but I do not think it too strong a claim to say that this feeling is as strongly developed in the Scot than as in any other people in Europe.

The Scot is intensely, sometimes admirably, sometimes irritatingly individualistic. The Highlanders naturally think of their countryside as of the essence of Scotland, so do the islanders. The Lowlanders will have none of this and maintain that Scotland is only truly Scotland South-East of the Highland line. But the divisions do not stop there. Each shire and district, even those least favoured by natural beauty or most spoiled by industrialism have their passionate local supporters. This is no unusual thing in England too, but it is not pushed to the extent there that it is in the smaller country of Scotland.

Edinburgh versus Glasgow; the Borders against the North; Galloway on its own; Aberdeen and Aberdeenshire even more on its own; the Highlands of the West; proud Perthshire . . . the list of individual divisions all passionately supported and argued about could go on indefinitely. Let me just conclude by giving one example of individuality pushed to an extreme. The inhabitants of the Shetland Isles consider themselves so much on their own that they do not even consider themselves, save administratively, as a part of Scotland. When they fly or sail to Aberdeen they don't talk about going to the mainland, but to Scotland.

Having proclaimed his individuality in his local loyalties as loudly as he can your Scot will at once team up with any other Scot from any other district if he hears a stranger impugning the beauty or quality of Scotland as a whole. I have even heard a Glasgow man defending Edinburgh, and an Edinburgh man defending Glasgow from outside attack.

This strong love for the actual country of Scotland is something deeply implanted in the Scot, and existed long before it became fashionable and enjoyable to admire the remarkable scenic beauty of parts of Scotland. Even when Scotland was agriculturally and industrially speaking a poor, even impoverished land, the inhabitants had a strong devotion to it. This devotion, nowhere more strongly expressed than in the border country aligning with England, certainly arose from the fact that Scots had by their own blood and effort won this land for themselves.

They did not win it for an overlord but for their own use and habitation. They were led first of all by the heroic Wallace and later by that truly extraordinary man Robert the Bruce, but it was in defence of and for the possession of their own homes and land that they fought at Stirling Bridge and then at Bannockburn. It is significant that throughout all the centuries during which Scotland was an independent kingdom the monarch was always known as King of Scots, not of Scotland. He did not own the land of Scotland, he was merely the first person in the realm of Scotland. Scotland belonged to the Scots, and the monarch was the King of Scots—or as in one famous instance of Queen Mary 'the Queen of Scots'.

All this was a long time ago, but its inheritance remains in the Scotsman's attitude towards Scotland. With all its imperfections, its occasional poverty of soil, harshness of climate and other physical drawbacks as compared with the warmer, richer Southern lands, it was and is his own land which he acquired and held by heroic defence still remembered in ballad and song.

Noble Prospects

Then, about a hundred and fifty years ago a new element entered in, this was the sudden perception by Western man of the beauties of romantic scenery. Until 1800 or thereabouts the average Southern visitor to Scotland, however agreeable he may have found the society of Edinburgh, was frankly disgusted by the scene of the Scottish countryside. He found the mountains 'horrid' (a favourite 18th century epithet for disagreeable surroundings) and most Scots could do

Scotland has many 'noble prospects'

no more than apologize for them: the Romantic Movement had not yet come in.

When poor Mr. Ogilvie in 1763 tried to defend the Scottish countryside in Dr. Johnson's presence, the best he could do, after rather lamely mentioning the good farming land round Edinburgh, was to refer to his country's 'wild and noble prospects'. This, of course, was asking for it. Sam Johnson's classic reply still reverberates down nearly two centuries:

"I believe, Sir, you have a great many. Norway too has noble wild prospects; and Lapland is remarkable for prodigous noble wild prospects. But Sir, let me tell you the noblest prospect which a Scotchman ever sees is the high road that leads him to England."

In less than a century from the delivery of that famous, but I cannot help believing, good-humoured buffet Dr. Johnson's own compatriots were, in holiday time, swarming on the high road to Scotland from England to enjoy precisely those wild and noble prospects of which the pawky Mr. Ogilvie spoke so timidly, yet with such shattering results.

The Romantic Movement begun in England by Wordsworth, Scoticized and made world-famous by Walter Scott, opened men's eyes all over Europe to the beauties of this mountainous, sea-girt little Northern Kingdom. It also opened the eyes of the Scots themselves to the beauties and attractions of their own land lying, as it were, at their own back doors. The Scots had always loved the land of Scotland as their own, now they were proud of it.

The Romantic Movement has passed, and is long out of fashion, but it has left some impressions on the mind of Western man which may well last as long as he does. It is unlikely that in our civilization mountains such as those in the Western Highlands of Scotland will ever again be referred to as 'horrid' just because they are large and difficult to circumvent. It is unlikely that islands which in the seasons of midsummer and autumn are to us so fantastically beautiful as the Hebrides will ever again be dismissed as desolate outposts of the mainland. At least, as long as Scotland is still inhabited by Scots, such a view will never be held again by the natives.

The Scot of today then loves the physical fact of his own land partly out of an atavistic sense of his possession of it by his own effort and partly because its beauty moves him more than does the beauty of any other country which even the most wandering of his tribe is ever likely to encounter.

This love for the varied beauties of his own country is one of the most sincere, unaffected and least sentimentalized of the Scotsman's emotions. It is discovered in all classes and ages. In the days of my boyhood in the early years of this century the privilege of enjoying the variety of the Scottish scene was confined to the wealthy or comparatively well-to-do ranks of Scottish society. No one, even at the height of the period when so much of Scotland was owned by rich sporting landlords, could enclose the moorlands and cut off the mountains. It did, however, take a certain amount of money to reach these remoter and more beautiful parts of the country.

Today all that is changed. The youth of Scotland, even from the poorest parts of the great cities, have discovered their inheritance of the land of Scotland and take advantage of it. And it is not only the young people who enjoy this inheritance. Cheap transport, the opening up of ways once forbidden, have had their effect on the middle-aged as well as on the boys and girls.

From May until late autumn (possibly the most tranquil and lovely season in Scotland) the countryside is filled with people from the towns, walking, climbing, angling, exploring, but above all, enjoying their inheritance of scenic beauty. It is one of the most heartening sights in the Scotland of today.

Chapter Six

The Burns Cult and Bonnie-Prince-Charleyism, etc.

The Cultivation of Cults

On the 25th of January, all over Scotland or wherever Scotsmen are gathered together in any part of the world, there are innumerable jamborees to celebrate the birthday of Robert Burns, the national poet. Sometimes these gatherings are worthy of the occasion. More often they are little more than whisky and haggis binges, with little if any relation to poetry. At the opposite end of the extreme they may take the form of inexpressibly boring and repetitive lectures (known as 'giving the Immortal Memory') in draughty town-halls uncheered even by the infusion of a cup of tea.

All over Scotland too the visitor will see and hear evidences of the cult of Bonnie-Prince-Charleyism. Inaccurate and highly sugared portraits of the Prince abound in most cities and are even used upon advertisement hoardings to promote the sale of a liqueur, the recipe of which he is alleged to have brought with him from France to Scotland. His effigy in stone beside that of John Knox, of all improbable people to associate with him, adorns the façade of a chain-store chemists in Princes Street, Edinburgh, along with other 'national heroes'. No concert of popular Scottish music is considered complete without a rendering of 'Will ye no' come back again' or some other Jacobite song or air.

Lest it be thought that the heading to this chapter and these two opening paragraphs are the prelude to a prolonged sneer at some of the more innocuous of my fellow-countrymen's sentimental indulgences, let me state, at once, that that is not my intention. There is a great deal to be said for annually celebrating the birthday of Scotland's unchallengeably greatest poet. There is also every reason why genuinely patriotic Scots should remember the last man to lead (and how nearly successfully) the Scottish troops of a genuinely independent Scottish army.

No, the trouble with the Burns cult when it degenerates into an absurdity which makes us the laughing stock of our Southern neighbours, and with the neo-Jacobite Bonnie-Prince-Charleyism when it becomes rancid with false sentiment is that both the originals of these cults were, in their own way, admirable men.

If Burns had merely been a rustic versifier of local Scottish talent, and if Prince Charles Edwart Stuart had been no more than the gew-gaw tartan figure which the advertisement posters make him out to have been, one might smile at the cults that have grown up around them in Scotland. One would not, as one so often is, be embarrassed by them or object to them.

THE BURNS CULT

Robert Burns, born of humble Ayrshire farming stock is not only Scotland's national poet, but one of the first writers of lyric verse that the British Isles have produced. He is something more; he is a poet of European standing whose words and sentiments have crossed the frontiers of all civilized languages.

To Scotsmen, however, he speaks primarily for and to themselves. His democratic (in the better sense of that much misused word) sentiments, his sturdy independence, his effortless yet forceful and often melodious use of the national tongue of Scotland, his unashamed amorous yet romantic virility and his personality make a strong and direct appeal to all Scots, Highland as well as Lowland. He was indeed a most delightful man. If I were given the chance to spend a day in the company of one great Scotsman out of the past I do not know whether I would choose Burns or Walter Scott—probably Burns.

All this makes Scotsmen feel that in a peculiar fashion they own Robert Burns in a way which few English people, save poets or professional writers, feel that they own Shakespeare. Burns's varied and generous nature has been interpreted and used by his fellow countrymen in practically every cause save perhaps teetotalism.

He has, of course, been enlisted in the popular front of man's equality with all other men. Even the Soviet ex-Premier, at the time of writing these words, has just been quoted in all the press of Britain as repeating Burns's lines "A man's a man for a' that". The Nationalists, naturally enough, have claimed him as their own special poet. The traditionalists, perhaps even Conservatives in politics, have seized hold of his Jacobite proclivities to say that at heart he was a supporter of 'king and country'. The extreme left has taken his Jacobinism at the time of the French Revolution as an indication that today he would be a Communist. In fact, whatever views any Scotsman holds (save possibly a detestation of strong drink and an inclination towards celibacy) it is possible to claim

Robert Burns's posthumous support for them.

And so it comes about that nearly every sodality in Scotland on the 25th of January can put forward a speaker who, in proposing the Immortal Memory, can use Burns as a peg on which to hang his own and his society's views about Scotland and the world. It also comes about that wherever two or three Scotsmen are gathered together anywhere in the world towards the end of January they can, if they feel so inclined, get together for a national 'unbend' on the excuse of celebrating the national poet's birthday. All this is a trifle ridiculous, but is it worthy of all the contempt which is poured upon it annually by the Scottish intellectuals?

When all is said and done, if we are going to have a national get-together day, the birthday of a poet is not a bad date to choose. As a man who makes his living by his pen I have always been pleased and rather proud that the largest public monument to any Scotsman (to any man) in the Capital of Scotland should have been put up to a novelist, Walter Scott. One may or may not approve of the preposterous architecture of this monument in Princes Street, but one does approve of the sentiment that erected it. One may not approve of the forms many Burns day celebrations take, but it is something to be grateful for that it is a poet's birthday which is being celebrated and not a politician's. Our Burns day binges may often cause the Saxon South of the Border some innocent merriment, but it would be no bad thing if they celebrated Shakespeare's birthday in an equally popular way. At least we could join in. Shakespeare is *the* poet of England, but we share his language with him, and with the English.

The one class of people in Scotland today who

perhaps have a genuine grievance about the Burns day celebrations are the living Scottish poets—and there are some very good ones too. Poetry, even the mere printing and publication of poetry, needs financial support today more than ever it did. Despite the undoubted reputation some of the modern Scottish poets have made for themselves, this is as true in Scotland as anywhere else. If only one tenth of the money annually spent in whisky, haggises and the hire of rooms to celebrate the birthday of a great but dead poet were to be given to the foundation of a magazine which could regularly display the latest Scottish verse, it would make all the difference to the living inheritors of the Burns tradition.

Bonnie-Prince-Charleyism

Bonnie-Prince-Charleyism, or sentimental neo-Jacobitism, is less defensible than is the Burns cult. It is purely sentimental; that is to say that it is an emotion that has no relation to fact in the present-day world. At least the speakers who pronounce or belch the words of Robert Burns at the annual celebrations of his birthday are emitting words that have some relation to life today. Alas! the lugubrious and occasionally melodious mourners over the failure of Scotland's last national rising, the insurrection of 1745, have no claims to be talking or singing about anything that is alive today. True Jacobitism in Scotland is, of course, long dead. The emotion behind it, the desire of the Highlanders to re-establish their ancient position in Scotland has not so much died as receded into the impossible. The desire of Scotland to return to her status as an independent kingdom may be put forward by some eager young

Nationalists and by increasingly elderly and, be it admitted, increasingly ineffective political theorists, but a venture such as the '45 is practically speaking as remote as Bannockburn.

The habit of sentimentalizing over Prince Charles's immortally remembered dash to regain the crowns of Scotland and England for his family (and, incidentally, to revoke the Union), his victories over the Southern troops with his Highland followers, his ill-advised retreat back into the mountains, his defeat at Culloden and his flight amongst the heather when no Highlander would accept the then enormous bribe of £30,000 for betraying him, began as far back as the late 18th century. It began when young Edinburgh ladies, and elderly Edinburgh clergymen, could without what the Hanoverian Government would have regarded as treasonable intent compose and sing poems and songs about the vanished Prince. They could do this without being accused of practical treason, not so much because the Prince was vanished as because the men whom he led, the Highlanders, were now utterly crushed or in thousands sent overseas.

The final absurdity of this form of sentimentality was reached when Queen Victoria, herself the grand-daughter of the Hanoverian George III, proclaimed herself 'a Jacobite'. Queen Victoria's devotion to Scotland was genuine and warm-hearted. She did much (in, as far as Scotland was concerned, a rather grim century) to restore the national self-esteem. But calling herself a Jacobite was really a bit thick. Though she may not have meant it to do so, it rubbed in the last element of fatuity into the cult.

In case it should seem that I am allowing myself to

be unduly irritated by the meaningless sentimentality of this cult, let me draw an analogy which every Irish and perhaps many English readers will appreciate. Suppose that the Easter Rising of 1916 in Dublin had failed in its ultimate effect, suppose that Ireland had after this brief glorious flash subsided into a torpid acceptance of British rule, and suppose that years, decades afterwards the drawing-rooms of Dublin were tinkling to the sounds of songs about the bravery of 'the boys of '16'. Suppose, finally, that in an Ireland in which the British still ruled, advertisement hoardings proclaimed the virtues of various drinks and other goods linked with the heroes of Easter in 1916. Would not every decent Irish stomach be turned?

That is all that the popular form of Bonnie-Prince-Charleyism is in Scotland today. The rising which Charles Edward Stuart led had as its proclaimed aim the restoration of the House of Stuart, and the character of the young Stuart Prince had much to do with the devotion to his own personal cause. The real fact behind the rising was that it was Celtic Scotland's last stand by the force of arms in its own independence. It failed, and its failure undoubtedly produced some poignant song, balladry and legend. The tradition of that inheritance is now debauched, deboshed and worthless.

This is not to say that anyone really interested in Scotland's past and in her last bid by force of arms for independence cannot follow the footsteps of the Prince in the Western Highlands and inspect his memorials with genuine emotion. But that is a very different thing from a 'Jacobite concert' in the 'tartan-lounge' of a modern Scottish hotel.

Other Cults

The heading of this chapter is—The Burns Cult, Bonnie-Prince-Charleyism, etc. There are not many etceteras in the line of cults that are not related to either Burns or Bonnie Prince-Charleyism. St. Andrew's Day, the anniversary of our Patron Saint, is much regarded abroad amongst exiled Scots, but frankly it is of little significance within Scotland itself. Despite the Scottish branch of the B.B.C.'s valiant efforts to think up something fresh for each St. Andrew's Day, few people in Scotland pay attention to it. It occupies about the same position in most people's minds in the Northern kingdom as does St. George's Day in England.

There are the historically genuine, and much enjoyed Border 'Common Ridings'. These take place annually each summer when the various Border towns appoint riders to inspect the boundaries of their respective parishes. Something in the same kind, of course, happens in various parts of England. In the Scottish Border towns, however, there is a real strong tradition based, of course, upon the ancient necessity of preserving the demarcation line between England and Scotland. This line has long ago been decided upon and defined. Nevertheless, something of the old Border watchfulness bursts out each summer in these Common Ridings. There is much junketing which sometimes lasts for days.

While on the subject of the Border line between the two countries, I cannot resist pointing out an absurd anomaly. The county town of that extremely Scottish shire of Berwick ought, of course, to be the one-time Scottish town of Berwick. Owing to the fact that this beautiful and historic town has passed from one nation to the other and back again, it has, as a result of some centuries old pact, *officially* settled down in England. The Border line runs three miles to the North of it. The result is that, though it is in character, and in the surrounding land of the shire which takes its name from it, Scottish, it is in law not allowed to be so. It is under the English legal system. It has a Mayor instead of a Provost and so on.

After the Union of the Crowns, but before the Union of Parliaments, it was in description considered a kind of no-man's-land. Treaties used to refer to 'the Kingdoms of England and Scotland and His Majesty's good town of Berwick upon Tweed'. This form of words continued even after the Union of 1707. It is said that it was used in the declaration of war against Russia at the time of the Crimea, but was dropped at the signing of peace. The official result has been then that this little Scottish-English town has, on paper, and for just about a hundred years, been continuing to wage an unequal struggle first with the mighty empire of the Czars and subsequently with the Soviets.

The cult, if it can be described as such, of the celebration of New Year's Day is distinctly on the decline within Scotland. The reason for its existence in such force at one time was the universal desire of North-Western man to hold a Midwinter Festival. Unfortunately the Reformers had clamped down on Christmas, which they considered to be a 'Papist relic' to such effect that (be it admitted with shame) this Christian feast had, save amongst Catholics and Episcopalians, almost been driven out of Scotland up to a time well within living memory.

Anyone whose recollection goes back to before the first World War can recall a time when all, yes literally all, the shops in any large town such as Edinburgh or Glasgow were open on Christmas Day if it did not fall on a Sunday. The same applied to all big businesses and offices which were not linked with England. But something had to be done to relieve men's spirits in the depths of winter. This something was done and with considerable gusto and style on New Year's Day.

Crowds would assemble just before midnight at some central place in any town where the chimes of a clock announcing the passing of the old year and the birth of the new one could generally be heard. At the significant moment all present produced at least one bottle of whisky and something little short of a Northern saturnalia commenced. This was followed by those still capable of walking, by the ceremony of first-footing. A dark-haired man bearing the present of a dark gift, sometimes only a lump of coal, would call upon his acquaintances. If his was the first foot to cross the threshold after midnight it was supposed to bring good luck upon the house for the rest of the year.

Junketing (with whisky at the price of 3/- or even 2/6 a bottle) continued till dawn. When day began it found empty streets, closed shops, and even closed public-houses in which not even 'bona fide travellers' could be served. But people were prepared for this. Every non-teetotal house was filled with the national spirit of Scotland, and as soon as the citizens could begin to stir again not only a hair of the dog which had bit them but whole handfuls would be applied. No lady of gentle culture would venture forth on New Year's Eve in any big city. Even on New Year's Day itself if she had to go out she would travel by cab, making careful arrangements beforehand that the cabby should be guaranteed to be sober.

New Year's Day is still celebrated in Scotland, but to nothing like this extent. The shops still close on the day itself and there are still rather formal junketings at midnight at such places as the Tron Kirk in Edinburgh. Two influences, however, have mitigated in abolishing the old, and on the whole, unsavoury Saturnalia. One is, of course, the price of whisky, the other is the entry of Christmas into public as well as religious life in Scotland. More than anything else the radio brought this latter effect about. When people sitting at home by their own firesides in Scotland heard not only England but the rest of Europe celebrating the birthday of Christ, they felt it impossible to withhold in this one little country—the knuckle-end of Great Britain.

Today, in the intervening stages between the passing of the New Year Festival in Scotland and the incoming of Christmas, people are rather getting the best of both worlds. Some shops and businesses close on both Christmas and New Year's Day. Some families manage to have reunions on both days. And when Christmas and Boxing Day, and consequently New Year's Day, fall about the middle of the week one gets the impression that as far as business is concerned much of Scotland is enjoying, what with the intervening Sunday, something like an eight or nine day midwinter holiday.

The cult of the tartan, in itself no bad thing, has already been partially dealt with. Though some Scots have entered into this cult with pedantry as well as over-enthusiasm, it is a cult mainly for export. We sell tartan, along with that curious local sweet Edinburgh rock, to our summer visitors. The cult of the kilt is naturally related to tartan cult and has been fully described and defended in these pages. A lamentable result of it, however, has been the way young women and girls have recently been encouraged to wear it. It is a masculine and martial garment, and looks ridiculous and unsightly on the female body.

There are other interesting cults of purely local or regional origin such as the Viking 'Up Helly A' festival in Shetland, or the setting of a lighted candle in the croft window on the island of Barra on Christmas Eve. This is designed to show hospitality to the Holy Family, should it be passing that night. Other Celtic countries have this practice also, but only in these Outer Islands is it preserved in Scotland.

The Better Side of the Burns Cult

Without question, however, the Burns cult is in Scotland the most lively, persistent and the one most likely to last the longest. Having begun this chapter on it I feel I should, in fairness, close by mentioning it and some of the better elements connected with it.

The Scot, whether Highland or Lowland, whether gay and easy in manner or dour and inhibited, is at heart a romantic creature with a taste for poetry if only he dare let himself admit it. Robert Burns, as the national poet, lets him admit it. The result is something that I omitted to mention in my earlier paragraphs, but which can provide a fitting conclusion to this section of this essay.

The really astonishing and really admirable thing about the Burns cult is the fact that it has made large numbers of the most unlikely Scotsmen learn by heart large passages of poetry. Nearly every Englishman can quote a line or two of the more celebrated 'tabs' from Shakespeare, but very few could do much more. Most educated Scots can do considerably more with their national poet. In nearly every gathering of Scots folk you will find people who can reel off line after line from Burns suitable to most occasions. There is one long poem, the celebrated 'Tam o' Shanter' which takes anything from ten minutes to quarter of an hour to speak aloud. I have continually been astonished by the number of ordinary men, not in the least connected with letters or poetry, who have been able to produce this poem faultlessly from memory.

It would be a good thing indeed if this capacity for appreciating and learning at such length the poetry of Robert Burns could open other doors too in the Scottish mind. It would be a good thing if the Scot could apply himself with the same diligence to the acquisition of some of the enormous legacy of English poetry and the smaller legacy of Scottish poetry other than by Robert Burns. Finally, it would be an excellent thing if he could be induced to take some practical interest in the by no means negligible body of Scottish poetry being produced today. But one can't have everything. The fact remains that the Scots knowledge and love of the poetry of Robert Burns is remarkable. For that element in the character of this paradoxical creature we should, at least, be grateful.

Chapter Seven

The Great City Rivalry

AN absurd, sometimes acidulated, but on the whole rather enjoyable element in Scottish life is provided by the rivalry between the two great cities of Glasgow and Edinburgh. It is a rivalry which extends far outside the city boundaries themselves and might almost be described as a rivalry between the whole of the East coast of the country and the West. To understand the Scot at home, with the exception of the Aberdonian who considers himself a race aprat, one must take into some account the place each one of them takes in this dispute.

Edinburgh, as people in the West frequently remark, may be the Capital of Scotland but Glasgow *has* the capital, that is in the sense of owning the money. In this claim the Glaswegians are, of course, correct. There are over a million inhabitants of Glasgow, and the city contains much rich and world-famed industry of which, of course, shipbuilding is the most celebrated. Edinburgh has little more than half a million inhabitants. There are in Edinburgh some flourishing and wealthy industries such as printing and brewing. The solid weight of Edinburgh, however, is provided by the professional upper-middle classes who as lawyers, doctors, bankers and administrators have their headquarters in the capital.

But there is much more 'to it' than this mere question

of money when one comes down really to considering this rivalry which preoccupies so much of so many Scotsmen's thinking time—particularly in the West. The real difference is a psychological one based on the history of the two cities and the manner in which they have grown up within the framework of the Scotland of the immediate past and the Scotland of today.

Edinburgh's past stretches back to well over a thousand years ago when the first houses began to huddle beneath the sloping protection of her prominent and dramatically placed Castle Rock. She was, even in the chaotic and vague beginnings of Scotland, one of the most important fortresses, cities and dwelling-places in the country, and for over six centuries she has been the Capital of Scotland. Our Kings, Queens and Princes once lived there and walked and rode in her streets. There is, even now, a touch of Royalty in the air of Edinburgh which has its origins in something much more antique than the associations of the present reigning House with Edinburgh whenever members of it come to Scotland.

Glasgow's remoter past too is by no means insignificant, but the echoes from that remote past of the great city of the West have been drowned by its roaring yesterdays and its still clamant present. In the Middle ages, Glasgow was the Cathedral city for the West of Scotland and possessed a famous University. Its main characteristic was an ecclesiastical and quiet studiousness. Lying by the banks of the then undredged River Clyde with a pleasant countryside all around it, it was the nearest approach that Scotland could then produce to such a seat of learning as Oxford. The Cathedral still stands, and is, of all those in Scotland, the one the least damaged by the rage of the Reformers. The famous University still, of course, exists in the heart of this great industrial district. For the rest, the old Glasgow has completely disappeared.

Glasgow's Great Change

In its place there has arisen in the last two hundred years a vivid, turbulent, shapeless, ever-growing industrial district rather than city which seems to the incomer to stretch endlessly down the banks of the Clyde and southward to comprehend other and smaller industrial towns. This change in the existence of Glasgow began as a direct result of the Union of Parliaments.

Former purely English colonies were thrown open to Scottish traders, and Glasgow, as the great port of the West, received that trade—mostly tobacco. Later when the Industrial Revolution arrived in Scotland the wealth of Glasgow supported it, and the River Clyde provided the ideal basis for its expansion. The shipbuilding industry of the Clyde became world-famous, and the phrase 'Clyde-built' was the highest praise that could be bestowed upon the construction of a vessel.

Wealth attracted not only more wealth but poverty. After the appalling tragedy of the Irish potato famine of the 1840s thousands upon thousands of starving peasants crossed the Irish Sea to seek work in the thriving industries of Glasgow. Workers also who were expelled from their various European countries as a result of the risings of 1848 also arrived in Glasgow. The once quiet little University and Cathedral city of the West became in little more than a hundred years something of a cosmopolis into which the dispossessed of the Western world poured for protection.

A cosmopolis, Glasgow may, in a sense, have become

but (and this is an important point) Glasgow and Scotland absorbed all these refugees and assimilated them. They may have retained many of their national characteristics and their religions, but they became sons and daughters of Glasgow, often more clamantly patriotic and civically conscious of the virtues of Glasgow than those whose forebears had been born there. There are no more obvious examples of this point than the Glasgow Irish.

The Glasgow Irish

The Glasgow Irish are so often discussed and so hotly debated over in Scotland that on that score alone it would be wrong to omit mention of them in any essay on 'Understanding the Scots'. They have, however, another claim to such a position, and that is quite simply that they have become Scottish, or at least Glaswegians, and have contributed much to the colour, life and quality of that most vivid city.

As Catholics, and most fervent Catholics, they have kept their religion, and as Catholics usually marry Catholics, they tended and still do tend to marry amongst themselves. They were at first, in the early and middle parts of the last century, employed only in the most menial industrial jobs. Their growing numbers and poorer standard of living increased Glasgow's slum problem. The blame for this problem it should be noted rested more on the shoulders of the owners of slum property than on the unfortunate poor who were driven to inhabit these hovels.

Still they stayed on, hovels or no hovels, and by the second generation, though they kept their names, had become Glaswegians. Some remained amongst the poorer and oppressed classes, others rose to high positions in the city. One recent Lord Provost was a 'Glasgow Irishman'. Some of Glasgow's best journalists and writers are Glasgow Irish. And the talents of these lively and vivacious people have added to the lustre of the Scottish legal system. They had become a part of Scotland.

But, for the ordinary douce or dour Lowland Scottish Glaswegian, their presence in the city did present a problem. No matter how ardently they proclaimed and felt themselves to be sons of Glasgow and of Scotland, their religion and their habit of marrying amongst themselves seemed to separate them from the more purely indigenous descendants of the old Glasgow.

Adding to this problem of apparent separation from the older natives was the Glasgow Irish habit of internecine strife. Not all those who had been driven from Ireland by the famine came from the South. There were Ulstermen and those who were Orange to the core as well. Thrown together in one slum district of Glasgow your Catholic from County Cork and your Orangeman from Belfast naturally tended on Saturday nights to pick quarrels with each other. In their native island they would probably never have met each other. But here in the squalor of a 19th century Glasgow slum it was a different matter.

The Irishman's most obvious failing is physical violence. This failing became encouraged and was spotlighted in the conditions obtaining in Glasgow until fairly recently. Whenever there was a fight or physical row going on in Glasgow it turned out that those with Irish names were at the centre of it. The Glasgow Irish were not prominent in other civic problems such as graft or prostitution, but whenever a broken bottle smashed over someone else's head you might safely bet that it was a Glasgow Irish hand that wielded it.

The Reputation for Gang Warfare

It was this habit of internecine physical warfare that gave Glasgow, in the earlier years and between the wars, the unwelcome reputation for being the city of razor-slashers and bottle bashers. The reputation was increased by the frequent journalistic mention of that poor district of Glasgow on the South bank of the Clyde known as 'The Gorbals'. There is something macabre about the sound and even the sight of that word in print, and those whose business it was to write up Glasgow crime in a sensational way were quick to perceive this. The very words 'The Gorbals' could in the 1930s send a shiver down the spine of respectable London housewives who read about this Glasgow district but who themselves may never have been North of Hampstead.

Nothing, save perhaps Edinburgh's indifference to Glasgow, annoys a true Glaswegian more than this horrific reputation that has been foisted on his city—the reputation for terrifying gang-warfare coupled with the name of the Gorbals. In point of fact, the Gorbals, a cosmopolitan district of shifting population, is rather better behaved than some other parts nearer the centre of the city. And as for gang-warfare, it does exist, but not noticeably more than in any other large industrial centre in Britain. Moreover, what people often forget is that unless one is actually a member of one of the gangs of rowdy youths oneself one is not only in no danger of being hurt but is extremely unlikely to see any signs of razor or bicycle-chain slashing, etc.

As has been said, apart from their tendency to physical violence amongst themselves, the Glasgow Irish are good and loyal citizens of Glasgow. They cling with devotion to their Faith, and in the miserable circumstances in which they found and sometimes still find themselves, they were and are as well controlled by their priests as is possible.

A Glasgow Irish priest recently told a story which in a somewhat double-edged way testifies to the fidelity of his race within Glasgow. He was going home one night through a March fog with his coat well buttoned up when he was stopped by a rough who, threatening him with a razor, demanded his pocket book. The priest was sufficiently alone and alarmed to undo his coat to begin to comply with the thief's demands. When his assailant saw from his collar whom he had been threatening he was aghast. He apologized and put his razor away. His Reverence, however, would not let it go at that.

"You and me must have a talk, my son," he said, "and now's the time."

He led him on the way to the presbytery to admonish him, and, in a true spirit of Christian forgiveness, offered the would-be thief a cigarette as they were walking along. His companion was much taken aback by the offer. "What, me smoke in Lent, Father! I would never do such a thing," he replied in shocked tones.

Other Celts not from Ireland but from the Highlands and Islands of Scotland poured into Glasgow after the evictions of last century, and it has been estimated that more Gaelic is spoken in the city by the Clyde than in any other town on this side of the Atlantic. Inverness, it is said, may be the Capital of the Highlands, but

Glasgow is the Highland capital. All this infusion, not only from overseas but from the Celtic North and West, of the dispossessed Highlanders has introduced an emotional as well as lively quality into the Glasgow character.

Mr. James Bone, author of *The London Perambulator* as well as part author of what still remains the best book on Glasgow, even though it was published over half a century ago, *Glasgow in* 1901, is a member of a distinguished Glasgow family, many of whose sons have made their fame far furth of Scotland. He tells a story of his boyhood in Victorian Glasgow. The Bones were members of a strict and extremely proper Presbyterian congregation. After evening service James's father used to bring home with him one of the most upright and apparently self-restrained Elders of the Kirk, called Mr. MacMillan.

The softening influence of the evening, combined with a hospitable glass of whisky, however, invariably produced a strange effect on this pillar of the Kirk. He began to indulge in reminiscences about the Highlands from where his forebears had come. Eventually the expressions of these memories and thoughts became too much for him. Tears streamed down his face as he bewailed the unfortunate state of his clan. "The landless MacMillans", he would sob before the startled younger members of the Bone family, "Oh, the landless MacMillans!" Such a scene on a Sabbath evening after Kirk would have been impossible in Victorian Edinburgh.

Edinburgh's Maturity and Golden Age

While Glasgow in one prodigious somersault changed

herself in a comparatively short time from a quiet little University town into the turbulent, active, emotional, shapeless lovable place she is today, Edinburgh did no more than go on grandly but quietly maturing. She had, it is true, grown a little since the beginnings of her existence a thousand years ago, but this growth had all taken place on the narrow strip of Castle Rock. It seemed, until halfway through the 18th century, that perched upon a rock, surrounded by water and swamps and other hills, Edinburgh had no room to expand save by building houses one on the top of the other. This, until 1760, the citizens of the Capital proceeded to do until Edinburgh became known as 'the tallest town in Europe'. Then a remarkable thing happened. Even though, by the Treaty of Union, Edinburgh had lost her status as the Capital of an independent country, she suddenly matured to an extent of which she had never shown signs before. But it was maturity, not, as in Glasgow's case, change that Edinburgh achieved.

The outward and visible signs of this maturity was the building of that most gracious piece of town-planning known as the New Town of Edinburgh. The citizens, tired of living piled up upon the rock, suddenly decided to drain the loch that lay to the North of them. They then started building in a wide, open, spacious and gracious manner in the wide and open spaces that were now lying free and open to them between themselves and the Firth of Forth. In the old days of piled up architecture it might have seemed that Edinburgh's motto was 'the sky's the limit'. Now it was 'the sea is the limit'. And a much greater scope that gave them.

At the same time at which this notable and lovely expansion of 18th century architecture took place there was another expansion in the spirit of Edinburgh of a different kind. She suddenly became the nursery of genius and the focal and central point of talent and learning in Britain.

This was the period in Edinburgh of David Hume, Adam Smith, Raeburn the painter. Burns was floated on his poetic career of fame in and by Edinburgh in the latter half of the 18th century. Walter Scott was born in the Edinburgh of this period. There were a host of other names, some still remembered, some half-remembered, and some now forgotten which were famous all over Britain at that time. The Capital of Scotland became known as 'The Academy of Europe' and a little later as 'The Athens of the North'.

Inevitably this high period of splendid building and apparently effortless superiority in learning, the sciences and in some of the arts had to come to an end. It did so slowly during the first half of the 19th century; but a tradition had been created. If that tradition declined later into a quiet and gentle 'professionalism' in the way of living, it was at least a tradition that remained.

How the Rivalry Arose

It may well be imagined what a sense of rivalry sprang up between these two cities—the one growing almost daily in wealth and size in turbulence and urgency of spirit, the other comfortably sitting back on a noble site conscious of a long historic past and a grand immediate yesterday. To add to the Glasgow man's irritation with this state of affairs, Edinburgh, with half the population within her gates of that possessed by the great city of the west, obstinately remained the Capital. Nothing could shift her from that position.

It was and is an absurd rivalry. In a small country such as Scotland men ought to be grateful for possessing two large cities so exactly complementary to each other. In what one excels the other fails, and *vice versa*. But no, the two cities, only forty miles apart, must continue their amusing but quite unjustifiable rivalry.

Your Glasgow man (after resenting the fact that a city so much smaller than his is the Capital of his country) most resents Edinburgh's apparent indifference to Glasgow's resentment. If you read certain Glasgow newspapers you would believe that Glasgow people had a kind of obsession about Edinburgh: they can never resist mentioning the place, usually accompanied by jeers about the town being "East-windy and West-endy". Also, it is alleged that Edinburgh in its subservience to the Southern Capital is 'half English'. To this accusation the Edinburgh people reply (if ever they so bother to reply) that Glasgow in accent, manners and aspirations is so thirled to Chicago that she is more than half American.

It is all very silly. Glasgow has the drive and the wealth and an extrovert, sometimes almost exhibitionist, way of behaving which provides Scotland with that commercial vigour which so distinguished her in the last century, and which is still important to her. Edinburgh, with its roots firmly planted in the past, gives Scotland a Capital worthy of one of the most ancient kingdoms in Europe. The two should recognize that between them they provide the qualifications needed for the two greatest cities in a small country upon the fringes of Northern Europe and leave it at that.

The difference between them could be described and

harped on endlessly. It is perhaps most succinctly summed up in something that has nothing to do with the people that inhabit either city but which is a purely physical or geographical fact. It is this:

The Clyde, it is said, made Glasgow. So also, in a sense, did Glasgow make the Clyde, for it was the enterprise of the city engineers in dredging the river bed which in the early part of last century converted a pleasant little stream into one of the most famous waterways of Europe. This same Clyde, rising in the moorlands and hills far above Glasgow, flows out through the great teeming city into the Firth and thus to the Atlantic and the West. The Clyde, Glasgow's river, is Scotland's gateway to the New World which Scotland at one time did so much to populate. The Clyde was, and to a lesser extent still is, Scotland's door to adventure and success.

Through Edinburgh there runs no River Clyde, but a quiet chuckling little stream which, having risen but a few miles outside the city, passes through a small part of its industrial districts but more notably through the classic environs of its 18th century New Town, and thus out to the North Sea. This little stream is, of course, quite unnavigable, but it is known as the Water of Leith. Leith (once a separate burgh) is Edinburgh's port and connects Scotland with her past—that is, Europe. That is the difference between the two cities. The one with its eyes on Europe rather than England (whatever the Glasgow people may say) has its roots deep in Scotland's past and never forgets that it draws its strength from those roots. The other, with its eyes upon the limitless horizons of the West, is conscious that it has been built upon yesterday's effort—and is proud of it. It looks to the future.

Edinburgh's New Vitality

And yet, since the war, there has been a curious shifting of balance. The Old Lady of Scotland who is known as Edinburgh has shown an astonishing exhibition of vitality. Whatever, in her massive, stone-built way, she may think about the future, she is certainly living, and living vitally in the present.

The most obvious example of this is the annually increasing success of the Edinburgh Festival of the Arts. I very well remember the gasp of surprise, the near-jeer that went up when in 1946, the year immediately after the war when the whole of Europe was exhausted, it was proposed to hold this Festival—and in Edinburgh of all places! We were told that no one would come to it, that Edinburgh's conservative chilliness would repel any who did arrive. Finally we were informed that, with half Europe still smouldering from the effects of the greatest war in history, it would be madness to attempt a gathering of European artists in so remote a place. The fact remained that, at a time when nearly everyone, with understandable lassitude, was saying 'no' to every suggestion, the Capital of Scotland returned a firm affirmative. In an era of 'abominable no-men', Edinburgh's 'YES' sounded out all the more clearly and distinctly.

The truth is that Edinburgh's antique position had been comparatively unshaken by the war. From out of her past she was able to draw deep reserves of quiet vitality. It is a vitality which shows itself in many ways. The Old Lady can still be maddeningly cautious and unresponsive when she feels like it, but she has, in the post-war years, provided a form of hospitality to the talents which are not only displayed at Festival time.

Edinburgh is now a delightful city to live in. It would be far too much to claim that it has restored any of the glories of its 18th century past, but it has levered itself out of the trough of complacent indolence which was its greatest weakness in the latter half of the last century and up to the time of the first World War. Robert Louis Stevenson, who both loved and hated his native city of Edinburgh (loved it for its grandeur and unquenchable character, hated it for its complacency) would, I cannot help thinking, like living in the Edinburgh of today.

Glasgow's essential vitality has remained unimpaired and, as displayed by the individuals you meet there, is as delightful as ever. She has, however, suffered a commercial shock in the withdrawal of importance from her heavy industries. Between the wars she, and her satellite towns, suffered most grievously from unemployment. She still can't think quite what has happened to her in the modern world and particularly in the Scotland of today. But she still provides for her inhabitants a lively and varied background which they love well. A true Glasgow man's love for his city, whether he be an indigenous Lowland Scot, a Highlander, an Irishman, or even a foreigner from further afield, is a genuine and heartfelt emotion.

'Doon the Watter'—An Edinburgh Tribute

Let this chapter be concluded by an Edinburgh-born man's tribute to the people and the city of Glasgow. It is a smoky, ugly, beautiful, optimistic, depressed, excited and immensely variegated place. Around it, and within easy reach of its humblest citizens, there is a beautiful countryside and seascape. Its people are as proud of its lovely surroundings as they are of their city itself—and that is saying a good deal. There is no more characteristic expression of the Glaswegians' love of the Glasgow country than is to be found in the summer trips down the River Clyde. Going 'Doon the Watter' it is called.

It is possible, by setting sail from the Broomielaw dock in the very heart of smokiest Glasgow, to sail out into and return from in one day some of the loveliest scenery in Britain. The West Highlands, and perhaps even a touch of the Hebrides, come right down to the mouth of Glasgow's river in that great and famous estuary, the Firth of Clyde. With all the noble beauty of Edinburgh's site, and with all the fine prospects across our own Firth of Forth, we have nothing like it in the East. And how the Glasgow crowds, the real proletariat (if that word is not too degraded by misuse) enjoy it!

The Clyde is the Glaswegian's own domestic river, and you will never see him to better advantage than when he and his family are at home enjoying themselves on it. Domestic is certainly the word. It is the family river of Glasgow; and it is the family that goes out upon it.

The children romp about on the deck on the outward journey through the city and by the dockyards. They run in and out amongst the deck-chairs. But these deck-chairs are occupied by their own parents and grandparents. Perhaps the children become a little tired as the long day's journey comes to an end, but it is because they are coming home, home, home to the Glasgow in which they were born and which is the background to their infant lives.

And if those same parents and elderly relations show

some quiet sentiment in their enjoyment of the journey home again, it is because they know that the lovely West Highland seascape and landscape through which the little boat has taken them on the day's journey has been all their own. It is their own because they are a Glasgow family. All this belongs to them in a way in which the countryside round London cannot be said to belong to the gayest and happiest Cockney crowd out on a Bank Holiday.

It is delightful to observe how the musicians who form the little travelling band on board ship play up to the sentiment and catch the changing moods of the journey 'Doon the Watter'. On the way down, past the shipyards and by 'the tail of the bank' where the river turns Southward and swells out into the great estuary, they play music suitable to the occasion. They play brisk popular airs while their audience is walking round the deck or queueing up for meal tickets.

Then, as the little ship turns backward on its homeward voyage, and as the passengers have by now enjoyed the full glories of the sight of Arran, the smaller islands, and some of the nearer West Highland hills, they change their music. The shadows of the hills lengthen. The sea takes on that peculiar and lovely calm of a late West Highland afternoon. The pleasant exhaustion of a day on the sea begins to induce an agreeable sentimentality. Now is the time for the musicians to play 'Roamin in the Gloamin' and 'Loch Lomond' and other airs which have remained deathlessly popular over many decades of 'Doon the Watter'.

Family groups, with the children now quietly clustered round their knees, sit shyly and not noisily humming or possibly singing the well-loved tunes as they take their last look for this particular day at their

'Doon the watter' or a day on the Clyde

own Clyde and Highland hills with the sun setting behind them. Then the clear pellucid water of the Atlantic gives place to the dark muddy waters of the Clyde River itself as they enter the waterway to their city. But have they ever left their city? Has not this journey down the Clyde been but an exploration of a garden which lies at their own back door? In enjoying this entrancing scenery have they not been only enjoying something that belongs to Glasgow? They would certainly think so.

That, as I have said, is a tribute of an Edinburgh man to but one part of Glasgow's life. Let it in ever so slight a way help to soften the absurd rivalry between Scotland's two great and complementary cities.

Chapter Eight

Puritanism and 'Hiving-Off'

"THE SCOTS," said one of the greatest and most distinguished of our compatriots within living memory "fornicate gravely but without conviction." I know exactly what 'Don Roberto', the lovable and remarkable R. B. Cunninghame-Grahame meant when he made this often quoted saying. I don't know that I would entirely agree with him. The shade of Robert Burns and a host of other joyfully amorous compatriots of 'Don Roberto's' and mine rise to deny him. But I know what he was driving at. He was referring to a habit, obvious amongst certain Lowland Scots, of taking their pleasures with a gravity which almost seems as if delight was distasteful to them.

This habit has been remarked on by many visitors to Scotland during the last century, but not before. A gravity of demeanour while dancing or drinking or merely sitting about listening to the band in a public place seems to have been a fairly recent development amongst the Scots. But, if it isn't taking the great Cunninghame-Grahame's lighthearted aphorism too literally, such gravity even in the act of love-making does not necessarily argue a lack of conviction.

This gravity of demeanour, of course, is a legacy of that peculiarly national blend of Puritanism which has both strengthened and bedevilled our race for the last four hundred years. It shows itself in the oddest ways, sometimes admirably, if a trifle depressingly, sometimes laughably and sometimes displays itself in a downright sour and displeasing fashion.

Before I go any further let me make it clear that by no means all, or indeed even the majority of Scots people, are deeply affected by this legacy of Puritanism. Indeed, these pages will have been written to little effect if the impression has been left that the Scot cannot enjoy himself with as much gusto and sometimes more gusto than the average Englishman. A thread of Puritanism, however, is in all of us; and when it shows itself it has an unfortunate habit of hitting the headlines in the press of all Great Britain to an extent quite in excess of its true value.

How often does one not read in every journal from Cornwall to Caithness a piece of information circulated by the news agency under some such heading "Scottish Church objects to the Duke of Edinburgh playing polo on the Sabbath," or perhaps "Scots kirk leaders shocked at Prime Minister's visit to Rome." What the newspapers which so gladly and so gaily disseminate these titbits of Puritanical scandal omit to mention is *what* Scots church objects, and what importance that church holds in the land.

The church which fulminates almost annually and with such large news results against any Sabbath-breaking in high places is not the official Presbyterian 'Church of Scotland' by law established but a small seceding body known as the 'Free Church' or more familiarly as the 'Wee Frees'. If the newspapers who give such prominence to the Free Church declaration were to explain this and its significance it would, of course, detract from the 'news value' of the story; so, not unnaturally, they refrain from explanation.

Let the present writer make it clear that, though he differs from the 'Wee Frees' profoundly on many theological points and most certainly upon the interpretation of their rigid moral theology, he has considerable admiration for them. They are the true inheritors of the 17th century Covenanters who, bigoted and unattractive though they may have been, were men of steadfast courage unto death. They knew what they believed in, and they never wavered. The present 'Wee Frees' know what they believe in and they never waver; for that they surely must be respected.

However much people in Scotland may respect them, or sometimes undeservedly laugh at them, no one here regards them as representing more than a minute proportion of the country's population and opinions. They are mostly to be found in the remoter West Highland and Island districts in those parts which did not retain the Catholic Faith. The Celtic temperament, if it is going to believe in anything at all, must believe definitely and not vaguely. After the Reformation the remoter districts of the North and West were left alone by the Church authorities in Edinburgh for over a century. Some endeavoured, but without priests, to keep the remnants of the beliefs of their forefathers. When priests eventually reached these people in the late 17th and early 18th centuries they were able to cling on to their Catholicism which they retain to this day.

In other districts to which the missionary priests did not penetrate the people were left without pastors until, in the late 18th century, a rigid form of Presbyterianism reached them. They welcomed its definiteness and became its ardent supporters. It is their descendants who are the 'Wee Frees' of today and whose occasional pronouncements are so gleefully seized upon by Fleet Street as the voice of Scotland. They represent considerably less than one per cent of Scotland's population and opinion.

'Hiving-Off'

Apart, however, from the passionate definiteness of their Highland Celtic opinions they do represent an important quality in the Scottish character—the love of 'hiving-off', that is separating into an infinity of little compartments of opinion. Let the reader be assured that he is going to be spared even a moderate compression of Scottish religious history since the Reformation. Since, however, this love of 'hiving-off' displayed itself most obviously in religious matters, some brief mention of it must be made in one paragraph.

As soon as the religious wars of the 17th century came to an end, and when the Presbyterian Church of Scotland eventually became established, 'hiving off' began in a really big way. By the end of the 18th and at the beginning of the 19th centuries there were actually between twenty and thirty differing sects of Presbyterianism. To the outsider the differences between these sects in faith or in behaviour might seem so trivial as to be almost imperceptible. But by the believers themselves these differences were most passionately marked, observed and upheld.

By now most of these sects have been absorbed into the national church or have died away under the general scepticism of the 19th and 20th centuries. The tendency, however, which produced them, that is the love of individual separation in belief and behaviour, remains most strongly in the Scottish character.

This love of separatism originates from what is, after all, an estimable trait in the Scot, his intense individualism, his dislike of being told what to think and how to think, his distrust of the herd, his lack of desire to go along with what the Americans call the 'bunch'. At his best the Scot does not give one hoot what the 'bunch' thinks of him; and one cannot but admire him for this.

Nevertheless, for anyone who attempts to organize vital opinion in Scotland, this tendency can be profoundly irritating. The smallest committee meeting must have its minority report; and even in that minority there is usually one individual who differs from everyone else including the minority.

This separatism or love of 'hiving off' is to be found equally in the Lowland and Highland temperament. It seems, however, to have its origin in a Celtic background. Religion apart, the Irish are almost as bad (or as good) at it as we are. It was only the appalling mistreatment of the Irish by the British, amounting to persecution, that ever united them to definite action. And when they were at their most united it was under the English-educated Saxon-landlord-born Parnell. One is sometimes tempted to believe that the only person who might lead the Scots to the expression of a definite national opinion would be a foreigner—an amiable and eccentric squire, let us say, from East Anglia; one of those English 'unusuals' who crop up in each generation to interest themselves in other people's national causes, and who usually do it very well.

To return, however, to Puritanism, which was the first subject of this chapter, this deep trait in the Scottish character was undoubtedly encouraged by the licence to 'hive off' which was granted to all Scots at the end of the 17th century and which was the eventual fruit of the Reformation. Each band of hivers-off seemed to attempt to outdo the others in inventing Puritanical regulations, the most excessive, of course, being Sabbatarianism.

Sabbatarianism

Sabbatarianism, save in remote North-West country districts, is much on the decline in Scotland today. Most Scots in middle-life, however, can remember a different state of affairs. They can remember a time in their childhood when even large cities such as Glasgow and Edinburgh seemed half-dead on Sundays. Few people issued out of doors save to go to either or both of the Sunday morning and evening services. The possession of a motor car was until the end of the first World War still the sign of a fairly well-to-do professional man, and most of these same well-to-do men would not then have used their cars for Sunday drives into the country.

All that is now completely ended. As soon as people have either gone to the morning church or have enjoyed their Sunday morning 'long lie-in', the streets and roads of Scotland are just as full of motorists, cyclists, pedestrians, hikers as they are in England. All save municipal golf courses are open on Sunday. There is bathing by the sea-side and in the lochs. The bona-fide travellers, as already explained, can enjoy themselves having drinks at seven-day licence country hotels all day. Here and there some regulation remains to remind one of the past, but in general it would be safe to say this: the two wars and the influence of radio have in the large towns and in most of the South of Scotland abolished the old Scottish Sabbath.

The Puritanism that made that Scottish Sabbath still stiffens the Scottish character in other ways, sometimes to good effect, sometimes, one cannot help feeling, lamentably. It is the legacy of Puritanism that gives the Scot such a strong sense of domestic decency. The better type of Scottish housewife keeps her home spick and span in the manner of the Dutch housewives whom one sees in the old paintings from Holland. The better type of Scottish father, even though he may not hound his family to the kirk as he did in the old days, preserves a patriarchal attitude at which one may smile, but which today is sadly lacking in many other parts of the world. It has its origins, even amongst non-kirk-goers in Old Testament teaching more than half-remembered. It may be a part of the legacy of Puritanism that gives the Scottish soldiers their dogged power of resistance and makes them amongst the finest troops in the British Army.

The 'Unco Guid'

On the other hand it is Scottish Puritanism that likes to pretend that everything in our larger cities is as respectable as the 'unco guid' would like to believe it to be. At the time of writing these words an announcement appeared in the press that the Edinburgh City Council had refused the offer of a bench or free seat for old people in the historic Grassmarket in the heart of the Old Town where there is still an undoubtedly large amount of slum-life still persisting.

The reason given to the would-be donor was that the seat might be used by 'undesirables'. By 'undesirables' the Council probably meant those pathetic down-and-outs who have recourse to the doss-house in the same

Grassmarket. No doubt these poor 'undesirables' might make a displeasing sight sitting in the open air (perhaps even drinking their concoctions of methylated spirits), and would in the eyes of respectable society be better hidden away in the doss-house. In short a form of social Puritanism would like to pretend that such sores on society's body do not exist. I am glad to be able to report that this decision to refuse a free seat for 'undesirables' has provoked some sarcastic comments in the press. The 'undesirables' may get their free seat after all.

It is Scottish Puritanism that gives so many of the faces of town-dwellers, even when they are supposed to be enjoying themselves publicly, that grim, unsmiling expression so beloved by the cartoonists. It is Scottish Puritanism above everything else which is responsible for an excessive sense of sin and guilt which has alas! haunted so many good Scots folk for the last four hundred years. There must be very few people left in Scotland today believing in the detestable doctrine of Predestination to Hell. The legacy of such beliefs, however, linger on.

If anyone, out of curiosity, would like to get a whiff of what this sense of sin once meant to the more strict Calvinistic Scots, let him read James Hogg's truly appalling novel *The Memoirs of a Justified Sinner*. The Ettrick Shepherd wrote this book in the early years of the last century when such characters as he portrayed in his grim story of 17th century Edinburgh had long disappeared. But he was nearer to them in time than we are and may well have heard tales of them. His book is a work of genius, and is all the more astonishing not only as the product of a country-bred shepherd but of one who was, to put it at its mildest, most certainly not bred in the Calvinistic tradition. James Hogg was not unduly oppressed by any sense of sin.

The Other Side

It would be inappropriate and wrong of me to end this chapter on so gloomy a note. I have endeavoured to be fair to what I consider are the better effects of Puritanism in stiffening the Scottish character, but I cannot conceal that it is an element in our national constitution which does not make much of an appeal to me. What I would like to point out to the reader and to remind him of is how successfully so many Scots have triumphed over this gloomy trait in their inheritance.

"*But gie me a cannie hour at e'en,*
My arms about my dearie O,
And warl'y cares and warl'y men,
May a' gae tapsalteerie O.
Green grow the rashes O
Green grow the rashes O
The sweetest hours that e'er I spend
Are spent among the lasses O."

It may have been the inspired heart of the Ayrshire farmer poet that in a sudden moment conceived these ever-popular lines, but he spoke not only for himself. He spoke for countless thousands of his compatriots who have shouted these and other of his songs, drunk or sober, into the teeth of the respectable Puritan tradition which has for so long tried to bind them down.

Burns was a genius, but he was a genius of the people and what he expressed found an echo in their hearts. There have been plenty of other minor versifiers in the Burns tradition who have expressed the Scottish gusto in love and in the taking of pleasure. Most of their verses are now forgotten, because their authors did not have their predecessor's talent, let alone genius. But they too in their minor way spoke for Scotland.

So did other people in by no means a minor way. Was there ever a writer with a more generous heart, with a greater taste for living than Walter Scott? Stevenson, with his tingling sensitivity, loved life and love and art and all forms of enjoyment. He lived at the very heaviest time of Edinburgh Scottish Puritanism in the last century, and he rebelled much against his surroundings. But he too, as he himself recognized at the end of his life, exiled in the South Seas, spoke for Scotland.

On the one hand one thinks of the undoubted Puritan tradition which has, here and there, strengthened, but more usually overlaid Scottish life. On the other hand one looks back remembering not only the famous names mentioned above, but others now nameless or forgotten who kept the flag of pleasure flying in Scotland.

There were the men of 18th century Edinburgh who upon a sea of claret and good sense floated happily through life, for the most part unhindered by the disapproval of their neighbours. There were the men who later on in the early 19th century provided the models for Christopher North's *Noctes Ambrosianæ*, including, it should be remembered, James Hogg himself, the Ettrick Shepherd. There were even the characters of Victorian Scotland, the eccentrics and the so-called ne'er-do-wells whom Stevenson recalls so unforgettably. The more one reflects on the past of Scotland's pleasure the more does one detect in it a virility which bids defiance to all rule which wish to crush it.

Scottish Delight

And today—one has only to look round and see that though the remains of the Puritan tradition may here and there constrict us we are not at heart a people with a distaste for or a distrust of pleasure.

Listen to the crowds at a football match in Glasgow or Edinburgh. Attend a Glasgow music-hall when one of their own favourite native West of Scotland comics is on the boards. Get yourself invited to one of the older Edinburgh dining clubs in the winter. Listen to the sound of the bagpipes; and finally, to return to a favourite subject of mine, either learn to do the Scottish country dances or just go and attend an evening on which they are being well and properly performed by groups of young Scots folk. If while enjoying or only observing during your attendance at any of these functions you keep your ears and your eyes open you will find plenty of evidence of the survival of the Scottish capacity for pleasure.

The blaze of Scottish tartan, the sound of the pipes, the swing and style of the Scottish dance, these and other manifestations of the vigour of the Scots capacity for pleasure are known all over the world. What is known also all over the world is the strong unbending character of the Scot which his Puritan inheritance has given him. The world too has alas! noted the effects on him when that Puritanism degenerates into a sour and jealous disapproval.

Here maybe we are at the heart of the paradox, the contradiction in the Scottish character mentioned so often in these pages. Puritanism can strengthen and can sour the Scottish character, but through it all 'cheerfulness keeps breaking in'. Scottish Delight has the last word.

Chapter Nine

'A Man's a Man for a' That'

THE title which Burns put above a set of swinging verses—and is quoted at the head of this chapter—is sometimes taken as a Scottish assertion and belief that all men are equal. This is of course nonsense, and Burns intended nothing of the kind. What he was, in a short and characteristic outburst of poetic gusto, trying to convey was his and his countrymen's belief in the equal dignity or worth of man in whatever circumstances he might be born. This is a favourite national theme. It arises from an estimable trait in the Scottish character, but, like many estimable traits, one can sometimes have too much of it, or, to put it another way, your Scot can sometimes harp on the theme a little too insistently. This is a pity, for Burns said it perfectly once and for all:

> "*Is there for honest poverty*
> *That hings his head an' a' that;*
> *The coward slave—we pass him by,*
> *We dare be poor for a' that*
> *For a' that an' a' that,*
> *Our toils obscure and a' that*
> *The rank is but the guinea stamp*
> *The Man's the gowd for a' that.*"

And so on for four other rollicking but triumphant

stanzas, concluding with that oft-quoted and heartfelt cry of hope:

> "*It's comin' yet for a' that,*
> *That Man to Man, the world o'er*
> *Shall brothers be for a' that.*"

Burns wrote these verses at the end of the 18th century when revolution was in the air, and when all over Europe men were looking to France in the hope that old order of privilege would there be dealt its final death blow. The Scottish poet, however, was not merely writing a set of contemporary political verses, he was expressing a Scottish sentiment which had been less articulately felt in his country for centuries before the French Revolution and which continued to be felt after the Revolution had been over and done with.

The Old Scottish Servant

Anyone who can remember the days of domestic service (after all they are not so very long ago) can recall in Scotland that attitude of respectful familiarity assumed by so many of the older Scottish servants. It was not a case of Jack being necessarily as good as his master, but of Jack, or rather Jock or Donald, being quite fearless in the assertion of the dignity of his position in the household. Servants in Scotland were never subservient or obsequious. They respected their master's position, but they equally respected their own. There are not many domestic servants of the old school left even in the houses of the great today, but the tradition of man's essential dignity in all classes happily continues to thrive.

Stories about the relationship between the old type of Scottish servant and master are innumerable. Some of the best of them are to be found in Dean Ramsay's *Reminiscences of Scottish Life and Character.* I can from my own childhood recall incidents which could illustrate this relationship; but as late as the mid-1930s I overheard a dialogue which was typical and as good as any that I could earlier remember.

An elderly Scottish Judge who had recently recovered from a cold was standing in the hall of his house in the New Town of Edinburgh on a fine spring day. He decided to walk the half-mile or so to his club in Princes Street and asked his manservant to give him his overcoat. The only reply he received was: "I'll call you a cab before I give you your coat, Sir." (He had called his master Sir for many years before the old gentleman's elevation to the Bench; there was no reason why he should now change to 'My Lord'.)

"But I don't want a cab, John. It's a fine day and I'll walk," replied the Judge.

"It's no fine enough for you to walk, Sir, I'll call you a cab."

"I intend to walk," said the Judge, now really rather irritably. "Give me my coat."

"I'll no give you your coat, Sir, and I'll no open the door for you until I've called a cab."

"Oh, very well," capitulated the Senator of the College of Justice, and sat down to await the cab.

An earlier story which has always pleased me was of a Forfar laird who one day stung beyond endurance by his manservant's bossiness decided that he must get rid of him. "I'm afraid you and I will have to part, James," he said after one stormy disagreement.

"Ay, laird," was the answer he got, "where are you gaun?" It never occurred to the old domestic that it might be he who should have to leave the house and lands where he had served for over forty years.

Another instance of a similar refusal by an old Scottish servant to accept dismissal is quoted by Dean Ramsay: An old coachman long in the service of a noble lady had given much trouble and annoyance, all of which he supposed to be the privilege of his position in the family. The lady eventually told him in the clearest terms that he must go. To this she received the quiet answer: "Na, na, my lady; I druve ye to your marriage, and I shall stay to drive ye to your burial."

Another servant faced with dismissal met the issue by the simple statement: "Na, na, I'm no gangin. If ye dinna ken whan ye've a gude servant I ken whan I've a gude place."

The dictatorial powers of John Brown, the humbly born Scottish servant, over Queen Victoria's household in the North at Braemar and even in her Court at London and Windsor are well known. Brown was not a very agreeable character, and not a good advertisement for the type: still he was an example of it.

These are instances of the 'a man's a man for a' that' principle in domestic service carried to its extreme. By no means all old Scottish servants were so high-handed, but they did, if they were of the true type, always maintain their own personal dignity as men and women in the families which they served. They considered themselves to be a part of these families, and though, of course, they had no delusions about their eventual position in relation to their employers, they were, let it be repeated, never subservient or obsequious.

No Obsequiousness

This lack of subservience and obsequiousness continues today amongst those in Scotland whose jobs are the more menial and humble. Domestic servants in private houses may be something of a rarity these days, but there must be those who in a public capacity still serve. Visitors from England and abroad to the Edinburgh Festival, for instance, often comment on the politeness without obsequiousness of our taxi drivers, porters, hotel servants and the like. One can honestly say that it just would not occur to these humbler servitors to behave in any other way.

This is the better side of the principle of 'a man's a man for a' that,' and is founded roughly on the idea that every true-born Scot is a gentleman, a relic maybe of the clan system as well as of the Burnsian principle. The less agreeable side of the egalitarian motto finds itself expressed in the graceless idea that nobody is a gentleman.

A lack of obsequiousness and subservience is welcome, but a contempt for fine manners merely because they are strange to them is a less pleasant element in some self-consciously proletarian Scottish circles. This is a type, of course, to be found in every country. In Scotland, however, with the capacity our countrymen have of going to extremes the type is more aggressive and graceless than elsewhere; fortunately he is rare. Most Scottish people from whatever social stratum they come have, if slightly slow and ponderous, agreeable and naturally gentle manners.

The Lad of Parts

There is one famous type of Scottish family which has often been mentioned in memoirs of the last century and in popular fiction and in plays. This is the humble family usually of country and often of Highland origin whose sons have gone out into the world and have won high places. Those members of such families who have remained at home usually manage to preserve an effortlessly modest demeanour about the success of their sons or brothers. Many a London gentleman up for the fishing or deer-stalking has been startled at the end of a few days to discover, maybe quite by accident, that the ghillie who attended him or the boatman who has rowed him on the loch is the father of a famous Harley Street doctor, an Oxford Don and a world-renowned scientist. Famous men have often come from humble circumstances in other lands. The Scots have a remarkable capacity for producing such famous men; they also have a welcome capacity for not boasting about it in the family circle.

This emergence of the great from some humble croft was very much a feature of 19th century Scottish life, before compulsory education was general, and when the native Scots' thirst for learning was general and to be found in all classes. In those days a 'lad of parts' from some obscure country farm or croft could, with the aid of the local dominie (village teacher) not only learn to read, but could get access to the classics of whatever branch of learning he wished to study. He would get a bursary (scholarship) to one of the four ancient Scottish Universities and be far ahead of his opposite numbers in England who then had neither his thirst for learning nor his opportunities for study; albeit impoverished study.

And impoverished it certainly often was. Many a Highland student would bring with him to Edinburgh or Glasgow or St. Andrews or Aberdeen a sack of meal and a cask of salt herrings on which he more or less entirely subsisted for the whole term. It was a sign of the pleasanter side of the 'a man's a man for a' that' principle that such youths were never disregarded by their teachers nor looked down upon by their richer and sometimes aristocratic fellow-students.

Nowadays, when everyone is taught to read and when talent of any kind from the Scilly Isles to Shetland is subsidised by the State, such native drive amongst the poor scholars of Scotland is reduced, or less necessary. It may continue as much as before, but the results of it are certainly less obvious. But the principle remains, and it remains a Scottish one. If nowadays a 'lad of parts' from anywhere in the British Isles can get his chance in the world of learning this is nothing new in Scotland. We did not so much invent such a system but we bred young men who made it possible.

The Clan System

Reference in passing has been made above to the well-known Scottish clan system. No chapter on 'a man's a man for a' that' or on the classes in Scotland would be complete without proper mention of it and what force it has today.

Let it be said straight away that there is a very great deal of romantic ballyhoo talked nowadays about the clan system and clan loyalty. But it is ballyhoo based upon something that existed in some strength up to the not so very distant past, and, when not sentimentalized or boosted for profit, still exists in the hearts of many Scots folk at home and overseas—particularly overseas.

Until about two hundred years ago the clan system existed most powerfully in the Highlands, and to a lesser degree amongst such famous Lowland families as the Scotts, headed by the Duke of Buccleuch. Under this clan system in the Celtic Highlands thousands of men bearing the same surname as their chief (Macdonald, Campbell, Fraser, etc.) owed him absolute allegiance. But it is important to note that it was a family rather than feudal allegiance. He, the chief, was the first amongst equals. The humblest member of his clan regarded himself as related to him.

The clan system was broken by the action of the Government after the failure of the rising of 1745. Its spirit, however, was much more seriously damaged by the behaviour of many, far too many, of the chiefs. These now found themselves no longer so much family potentates on a large scale as just ordinary landlords owning vast tracts of mountain and moorland. Up till then this land had belonged to the clan, and the chief merely administered it. Now he was as much a possession of it as was any English squire of his broad acres in the South.

Alas! Paternalism in many cases gave way to greed. The chiefs found first sheep then deer forests more profitable than human tenants. And even when those tenants bore the same name as they did and were often blood relations, the chiefs were far too often amongst the worst of those who evicted or at least connived at the eviction of the Highlanders.

By no means all of the chiefs behaved in this way. The Macleods of Dunvegan in Skye and the Frasers of Lovat were, amongst others, notable and praiseworthy exceptions. But as regards many of the rest it is not a pretty story, and is unpleasant to dwell upon. But it must be mentioned, for it is the recollection of the behaviour of so many chiefs in the past during the sad and bitter period of the clearances that makes the contemplation of some of the modern ballyhoo about clan loyalty not only sentimental but distasteful.

The fact remains that, though sadly depopulated, there are various districts in Scotland associated with various clans and in which you will still find that a number of the crofters bear the same name as the chief. The fact also remains that all over the world, particularly in the new world of Canada and the U.S.A., there are countless Scotsmen drawn to each other by the simple fact that they still bear the same Highland names. They still like to feel related, no matter how distantly, but still related to each other.

Overseas there are the most active clan associations. These are often composed of men who, descended from emigrants, have now grown wealthy and like to come to Scotland to visit the lands and the clan-lands of their forefathers. Perhaps, with their transatlantic capacity for display they make rather too much of a fuss about it all—too much of a fuss, that is, for those native and still resident Scots who remember how the clan system broke down. But they do no harm; they bring some dollars, and some warm hearts to Scotland.

Clan rivalry is a thing of the past. The intense hatred, for instance, that once existed between the Macdonalds and the Campbells is remembered only in a joking spirit. But the Campbells who come from abroad still like to feel that they are somehow related to the greatest Campbell of all, the Duke of Argyll, and the Macdonalds to whatever one of the Macdonald chiefs with whom they believe themselves to be connected.

All this is pleasant and agreeable enough. It is a harmless way of remembering "old unhappy things, and battles long ago". But perhaps there is something more to be said for the memory of the clan spirit as it exists today. A man bearing one of the great and famous Highland names of the past can feel that, no matter how humble his circumstances, he is of a great inheritance. He is, along with the descendants of the 'Chief' who has the same name as him, as well as many other distinguished bearers of it, 'a man for a' that'.

The 'Aristocracy'

The chiefs are, of course, only a part of what it is perhaps a little too charitable to call the native aristocracy. Outside the old Highland line and away from the lands that still have some connection with the clans, either historically or by the presence of those bearing clan names, there are plenty of other landed proprietors of ancient but not Celtic descent. Some of these bear names or titles as sonorous and as historically worthy as those of the Highland chiefs. Buccleuch, Montrose and Douglas are but some of these.

For the most part, however, the landed aristocracy of Scotland, whether Highland or Lowland, that has kept its land and a certain amount of money has become thoroughly anglicized. Some families, the Strathmores, for instance, have been marrying into English families for two hundred years. Though their family seats, from which they take their titles, are situated in Scotland they have joined the ordinary ranks of British (some of them would even call it the English) aristocracy. They send their sons to Eton and Oxford or to other English public schools and Cambridge or into crack Southern regiments. The products of such education are certainly agreeable enough. Indeed there are few pleasanter people to talk to than the well and comfortably educated younger members of the upper classes in these islands who have adapted themselves to modern society without any social complexes of any kind. But in joining this agreeable freemasonry of the British Upper Classes, the Scottish aristocracy have for the most part abandoned their nationality.

For the most part! But there are and have been honourable exceptions, such as the late Duke of Montrose, the late Duke of Argyll (who with all his eccentricities was a Scottish and European rather than British aristocrat), the present Duke of Atholl and R. B. Cunninghame-Grahame, a fiery and passionate Scot if ever there was one, and one or two others. Mention should be made of the Earl of Crawford and Balcarres who really does not only live in but works for Scotland in the Arts. Oddly enough he also holds an English peerage under which he sits in the House of Lords. He is Baron Wigan, and has been known to call himself the original Wigan peer. A near neighbour of mine, who has some of the best blood in Scotland and who still keeps his land, prides himself on speaking Scots in the broadest fashion, and is not unlike one of the more eccentric lairds out of a Walter Scott novel.

These are exceptions. The ordinary Scottish aristocrat of noble name or of long pedigree is undistinguishable in accent, speech, manner, attitude of mind from his English counterpart. Apart from his territorial associations with the land that gave his forefathers their birth and their possessions, he sometimes keeps up 'Scotch customs' in his home or in his public life. If he lives North and West of the Highland line he will usually wear the kilt. He sometimes keeps up associations with the Church of Scotland in his neighbourhood, though he will (if he is a churchgoer) probably attend the Church of England with his English relatives when he

In joining the agreeable freemasonry of the British upper classes the Scottish aristocracy have abandoned their nationality

is South of the Border. He is a member of one or more of the ancient Scottish orders or foundations such as the Knights of the Thistle, the Royal Bodyguard of Archers, etc. But if you heard a congregation of one of these orders talking together you would think you were amongst a group of amiable upper-class Englishmen.

For a Scot who looks across the Irish Sea there is one odd thing about this almost complete anglicization of the Scottish aristocracy. The Anglo-Irish, though in blood, religion and custom cut off from the native Irish, 'went native' in a few generations. Some of the most characteristic Irishmen with all the stage qualities of the Irish are of Anglo-Irish or 'Ascendancy' origin. Not so the Scottish aristocrat. His associations with England have made him 'go native', but 'go native' in an English fashion.

Other Classes

The upper middle classes, the professional men of wealth in Edinburgh or the rich industrialists of the West, were in the days of my own boyhood consciously Scottish in speech, manner and outlook. As more and more of them, however, are being sent into England to be educated at various English public schools, this Scottishness is often rubbed off them in boyhood. It is nevertheless interesting to note how many of them revert to type when they come back again to work in the professions or in the paternal and family businesses.

The shopkeeping and intermediate class in town and country could, of course, never be mistaken for anything else but Scots. The labouring or industrial classes when not of foreign extraction are superbly and unselfconsciously Scots. It is they who are, in a sense, the true gentry of Scotland. In the country, particularly in the Highlands, their manners could not be rivalled by the finest courtiers. In the towns, where industry has overlaid their natural way of living, the more graceless side of their nature tends to emerge, but it is in the country and the country folk that you will find men who are men 'for a' that'. It is in meeting them that you will get to know the inner meaning of Burns's fiery and rollicking poem.

Chapter Ten

Nationalism

ON Christmas Eve, 1950, the Stone of Scone, sometimes known as the Stone of Destiny, was removed at night from Westminster Abbey in London to which place it had been taken from Scotland by Edward I after his victorious invasions of Scotland before Bannockburn seven centuries earlier. Those who removed the Stone were some young and ardent Scottish Nationalists from Glasgow University. They took the Stone back with them to Scotland by devious and circumspect means. It remained hidden there for about six months until on the advice of some highly placed authorities in Scotland it was deposited on the altar of the ruined Cathedral at Arbroath, and the public informed. The police at once swooped upon it and removed it back to London. It is now restored to Westminster Abbey surrounded by the protection of radar guards which, in the event of another attempted removal, will ring alarm bells in all Scotland Yard and, it is said, in Buckingham Palace itself.

Until this truly sensational event it is probable that less than half of one per cent of the electorate in England had ever heard that there was such a thing as a Nationalist movement in Scotland. Outside England and on the Continent of Europe no one except a few literary-minded individuals who had read modern Scottish poetry and journalism could have had the faintest idea that such a thing existed. And yet, while the Scottish Nationalists at home certainly did not appear to get much practical political support, it is true to say that in various forms, not only political, Scottish Nationalism had been a number one topic for at least twenty-five years before 1950.

It is not my purpose here to discuss whether or not it was good taste to remove a Stone historically associated with the Coronation from a famous church on Christmas Eve—a matter which much shocked English opinion, though some sections of Scottish opinion pointed out that putting 'stolen property' in a sacred building was to invite 'sacrilege'. Nor, beyond attempting to explain the political failure up-to-date of the Nationalists in contrast to the attention they have aroused, do I intend to discuss the practicability of their proposals. I do wish, however, to point out that this daring removal of the historic Scottish Stone of Scone from the heart of the English capital drew literally world-wide attention to something unexpected which had been going on in Scotland for some time, and I would like to explain the significance of that something.

In the 1920s young Scotsmen came back from the first World War fought to defend the rights of small nations and looked round on their own country with some dissatisfaction. Europe had had its complacency shaken to its foundations. The Scotsman's 19th century complacency with his country's position as a unit of Britain slowly but inexorably being absorbed into England also received a bad jolt.

Ireland had just gained her freedom. We were not in the same case as that unhappy island. We had never been persecuted; we, so it seemed to these young men, had suffered a more ignominious national fate. We were enduring slow and comfortable extinction—but nonetheless extinction. Scotland, thought these young men, should express herself as Scotland, an ancient kingdom, and a country with its own rights.

The Scottish Renaissance

They began to try to express Scotland through themselves in various ways. Artistically, and particularly in writing, there was an upsurge of purely Scottish production meant for Scottish consumption. We were tired of plays in the Sir James Barrie tradition in which, whimsically or farcically, Scots people were held up (at immense profit to the author) before London audiences as amusing or incomprehensibly dour barbarians. We were tired of tinkling sentimental verses in the neo-Jacobite tradition passing for Scottish poetry. We thought that there was a possibility for native music on a scale rather more worthy than the composition of Scottish Country Dances or the rescuing by such amiable ladies as Mrs. Kennedy Fraser of Hebridean songs. At any rate we (or rather they, for I was both abroad and a little too immature at that time to join in) tried to speak for Scotland, and particularly speak through the printed or dramatically spoken word.

It was all very exhilarating. This was the time in which James Bridie, the pseudonym chosen by a Glasgow Doctor of Medicine—O. H. Mavor, was writing his plays for 'The Scottish National Players'. Later his name became much known in London, England and further abroad. It is significant, however, of the impetus behind his work that some of his best plays such as *Gog and Magog* were intended for Scottish audiences and have not gone down well in London.

This was the time when Eric Linklater was, against a Scottish background, becoming known as a Scottish novelist—though the world rather than Scotland was his theme and his oyster. This was the time when Neil Gunn first became known as a novelist. And this also was the time when Compton Mackenzie first came back to live and write in Scotland, drawn more insistently to the land of his forebears than George Moore had been a generation earlier, to Ireland.

In a chapter such as this one could clutter up the pages with lists of names, some well-known, others of only local celebrity. This would be boring, so let us conclude with the name of a very remarkable poet who in his verses seemed to the young men of the time to crystallize the whole movement known unfortunately and rather pompously as 'the Scottish Renaissance in Art and Literature'. This was Hugh McDiarmid who, with his lyrics in the old Scots tongue and his great poem *A Drunk Man looks at the Thistle*, seemed to some, even at this latter date, to challenge the supremacy of Burns.

McDiarmid, now halfway through his sixties, remains the inspiration of all the younger poets writing in Scotland today. Either as McDiarmid, in which name he writes his poetry, or as C. M. Grieve, his own name which he uses for his highly lively polemical writing in prose, he is known all over Scotland. How well he is known in England I can never quite make out. I don't think he would care very much. He relishes much more a reputation which he has won for himself amongst the *literati* of the Continent of Europe and in Ireland.

The medium in which McDiarmid and his followers write poetry is mostly that of Broad Scots, or the Old Scots Tongue. Undoubtedly they are at their most effective when using this speech. Some plays, particularly Alexander Reid's *Muckle Mou'ed Meg* and Robert McLellan's *Jamie The Saxt*, already referred to, have also and with considerable success been presented in the same language.

This led a development in the Scottish theatre which would have truly astounded an earlier generation. From the time of John Knox until after the first World War the theatre was either forbidden to Scots folk or was an exotic brought into the larger towns by touring companies from London. There had been no real, live native theatre in Scotland since the Reformation. Suddenly the loosening of Puritanical bonds after 1919 released the Scotsman's native love of acting. The lid was taken off the pot primarily by that remarkable movement known as Scottish Community Drama. Within a few years, from John o' Groats to the Mull of Galloway and even further on the islands, there sprang up hundreds upon hundreds of village and small town dramatic societies in which (and you have to be a Scot to realize the significance of this) the minister's wife often played the leading lady.

It would be too much to claim, save here and there, much artistic merit for these productions, but it did make Scots folk all over Scotland conscious of and interested in the theatre and the native theatre. The genius of James Bridie and the talents and hard work of the Scottish National Players furthered this newly aroused dramatic consciousness of the Scot, and directed it into worthy channels.

There exists today in Scotland an ardently enthusiastic Repertory Theatre Movement which has branches in most big towns. Not all these branches flourish financially, and the standard varies. But they exist (and such a state of affairs would have been thought impossible a *quarter of a century* or thirty years ago), and they exist mostly for the projection of the Scottish theatre—plays by Scottish authors acted by Scottish actors. That they are able to keep their heads slightly more successfully above water than do their English equivalents is because they are able to present to their patrons what they cannot get on Television or the cinema. By this I mean not only flesh-and-blood, live theatre, but theatre that is truly national.

Political Nationalism

Alongside this literary and artistic renaissance in Scotland there also sprang up a political movement. In the 1920s the National Party of Scotland was formed by a Duke, a poet, a novelist, a miner, some students and a handful of ordinary Scotsmen drawn from the working and professional classes. This Home-Rule Party proceeded, and with considerable lack of success, to contest various Parliamentary elections. The only Nationalist member returned up to the time of writing was in 1945.

Yet, in 1949, Scottish Convention, a kind of self-appointed Scottish Parliament for discussing Scottish affairs, was able to announce the distinctly startling result of a nation-wide plebiscite known as the National Covenant. The Covenant was a sheet of paper circulated with considerable assiduity throughout the length and breadth of Scotland and in the Islands. Those who signed it were asked to return it to the central offices of the Covenant movement, and in signing it they pledged themselves to "do everything in their power to support a Parliament in Scotland for Scottish affairs within the framework of the United Kingdom and in full loyalty to the Throne".

Over two million signatures were obtained for this declaration in Scotland. This figure was well over half the electorate of Scotland. Making all due allowances for those who were drunk or who signed twice or were otherwise incompetent the figure remains impressive. It proved beyond doubt that a very large number of Scots people were dissatisfied with their country's position in the United Kingdom and in various degrees of vagueness or of certainty approved of a measure of Home Rule.

How do the Nationalists account for the contrast between their conspicuous failure in Parliamentary elections and the figures of 'the Covenant'? They claim that under the two-party system such a general fever of excitement is engendered on the necessity of kicking one party out of power or kicking it back again that all other issues, even domestic Scottish issues lying at our own doorstep, take second place. This is an admission, possibly not a completely damaging one, but an admission all the same. It is an admission that while many Scots feel deeply about the subservient position into which their country has, politically speaking, been forced during the last two centuries, they do not feel strongly enough about it to refrain from voting Conservative or Labour instead of for the Nationalist or Home Rule candidate.

And so the matter rests. Quite apart from the hard core of enthusiastic Nationalists and Home Rulers in Scotland it is obvious that there is a vague and ill-defined irritation, even anger, about English and above all London control of Scottish affairs. The Scottish members of Parliament are, at the time of writing, a pretty poor lot and are generally regarded as such in the country. One may well blame the Scottish electorate for putting them where they are, but one must remember that these members are little more than local figure-heads put forward by one or other of the two party machines, and as often as not selected particularly for their docility to the Party Whips.

In times of prosperity or comparative prosperity and when there is no unemployment, people in Scotland in a grumbling sort of way are prepared to put up with this. Should things ever get hard, bitter and uncomfortable again in the Northern Kingdom, Westminster might not find it so complacent.

Complacent—that is the unfortunate epithet which has for so long bedevilled Scottish life. In the 18th century we sold our nationality in the hope of creating a real new country called Great Britain, and under the impression that we were joining England in, as far as national rights went, an equal partnership. Slowly but surely we have found our nationality being swallowed up in the digestive tract of the amiable and entirely well-meaning larger partner. It was, as the opponents of the Union foresaw at the time, inevitable. We have only ourselves to blame. It is from this cause that arises that national Inferiority Complex referred to in lighter terms in the first chapter.

Will the Scottish Character Survive?

And yet . . . and yet it is unlikely that the Scottish character described in this short book, I hope in not too great seriousness, will disappear into the amorphous conception of Great Britain. Apart from all the innumerable differences, racial, linguistic, religious, humorous and of behaviour that exists between the English and the Scots there is something else which gives one hope of national survival. It is the spirit that is abroad amongst our young people today. It is the spirit (and I do not use these words in a jingoistic or chauvinistic sense) of the New Nationalism. Young people in Scotland today in their writing, in their art, in their talk and sometimes in their politics are conscious of being Scots first and foremost in a way in which they were not when I was a boy.

Is this just a flash in the pan? Is it no more than the last squawk of the national chicken before its throat is cut? Will television and the cinema, not to mention the tabloid press circulated all over Scotland and now controlled from Fleet Street, roll out and obliterate all the differences between the Northern and Southern Kingdom save perhaps for a few provincial peculiarities?

No one can answer these questions except the children of Scotland who are going to be the young people of this country in the not so very distant future. They look a very healthy breed of children to me. They have an independent air about them as well as a healthy look. Perhaps they will be able to keep their national as well as their individual independence in the future. Who knows?

I am well aware that in this last chapter I may have hinted at or even expressed views with which many of my countrymen would disagree. But then that is one of the things that is most important to remember in 'understanding the Scots': we most of us disagree with each other. We are, above everything else, a race of individuals.